A Year with Poetry

Tea... ...s ...e ab...t...

Edited B...

...ty of Glouce... ...re
...e, 56 East ... Dock Road
...4 6JE ...
...22... ...

Centre for Language
· CLPE ·
in Primary Education

Contents

1 **Making poetry matter**
Michael Rosen

2 **So you may ask yourself, how did I get here?**
Ally Mullany

3 **Juicy Bits: developing a taste for poetry**
Andrew Lambirth

4 **Two children**
Colette Morris

5 **A Poetry Journal: a year with Year 6**
Varina Emblen

6 **Not quite Tennyson**
Julia Gatt

7 **Joining the Poetry Club**
Jenny Vernon

8 **A personal journey**
Maria Maguire

9 **Children performing poetry**
Linda Mariani

10 **Be a Poet**
Jimmy Symonds

11 **Ways into English with bilingual children**
Michele Rowe

12 **Organising a poetry week**
Varina Emblen

13 **A year with poetry**
Myra Barrs

Making poetry matter

Michael Rosen

This book is the story of a year when a group of London teachers and I met to work with poetry. The book itself is written by the teachers; this is my introduction to how the year began.

I am not a classroom teacher. I am someone with a passionate belief that all of us, no matter how old or young, have the ability to reflect on who we are, what we do, where we come from, what others do to us, what might happen to us, what we hope for, what we see and hear and what we share. These may be our failures and successes, fears and losses, absurdities and anxieties, shames, boasts, amazements, mysteries, yearnings and much, much more. Not only do we all have that ability, but it is a human right that we should have the opportunity to use it.

The idea that all children can write poetry is a fairly new one. In saying that, I am overlooking the classical way, inherited from the Greeks and Romans, which was instruction in 'measures', the imitation of fixed metrical forms. Even so, this way of teaching was for many centuries restricted to a tiny minority of young people. It is not until the 1920s that ideas start emerging that all children can be creative and that this creativity can be expressed in words and poetry. By the 1950s, when I was at school, 'poetry lessons' could be a matter of learning and reciting poetry individually, 'choral speaking', comprehension questions on individual poems and, yes, writing poetry.

Since then, we have seen a boom in children's literature, part of which has included a phenomenal growth in the amount of poetry being written and published for children. A book like Allan Ahlberg's *Please Mrs Butler* is a permanent best seller, there is a constant flow of schools' radio and TV poetry programmes, schools all over the country have poetry weeks, visits by poets, poetry competitions and the like. Every year, the W H Smith's writing competition attracts thousands of entries and there are many other poetry events and competitions happening all the year round. As part of this huge output of effort and thought, there has grown up a little industry of books intended for teachers to help them teach poetry. I've written one myself - *Did I Hear You Write* - and in part, the book you are now reading comes out of that one. The problem is that these books tend to follow a pattern, something like this: 1. Here is a poem. 2. You could write a poem like that.

The reason why such books are popular with many teachers is that the process from 1 to 2 seems to work. You can open the book at any page and teach a lesson. When 1 is a poem that the children are interested in, and there are enough children in a class willing to co-operate with the teacher, then 2 will happen. Surely then, this is 'effective teaching'? Something happens: it works? Yes and no.

I wouldn't for one moment want to say that these books and the process I have described are worthless. Rather I would want to ask, how can it be richer, deeper, and of more value to everyone involved?

What is Poetry for?

This means raising that old chestnut, what is poetry for? As I see it, the value of poetry is that it should *matter*. It should matter first to the writer and then to the reader. It can matter in many different ways: because it deals with important things for that person; because it shows aspects of the usual and everyday and makes them appear new; because it unmasks everyday things and shows how they really work; because it deals with the different ways in which language itself is used and shows these uses to be at times absurd, dangerous, silly, musical, rhythmic; because in a very fundamental way, the person who embarks on writing about things that matter learns that language is a resource available to every single one of us to use and to play with in order to suit the situation we're in.

What modern poetry offers us is an almost limitless range of possible tones, themes, sounds, voices, forms, patterns and rhythms. In other words, central to poetry is play. Play needs saving from all the abuse it has had thrown at it over the last few years, as it is the basis of learning. Play is the open-ended process of trial and error, without worry of failure or derision, that enables us all to grow and learn. Even the brain surgeon, that analogy so favoured by theorists wanting to give an example of high skill acquisition, will have spent many years playing. I know - I was once a medical student and I can assure you, medical students spend years in dissecting rooms making mistakes with scalpels and scissors and enjoying the 'oh whoops' moments. Then again, infants between the ages of just a few months and say, three or four, will spend hours and hours

babbling and playing with the raw sound of the language(s) around them. We are all as entitled as infants to play with speech and to play with language on the page.

For some this is a frightening and retrograde step. Those historic forms like the ballad and the sonnet or the couplet seem to have been beaten into retreat and now all that is left are word-games and 'chopped up prose'. I sometimes wonder why this is a problem. Even if 'free verse' were chopped-up prose (and most of the time it isn't) why should this matter? If someone wants to chop up prose into short lines, then this doesn't seem to me to be evil or sinful. It might, after all, make it easier to read out loud.

Perhaps the problem lies in the word 'poetry'. It seems to some that this word should be preserved to refer to certain very specific language patterns and that it should exclude others. The snag is that no sooner do such people say what should be in the poetry club and what should be out of it, than we can all find exceptions. After all, when the King James Bible was delivered in 1611, it contained what were in effect some of the most amazing free verse poems ever published, like 'The Song of Solomon'. And John Donne would not have thought of his sermon 'No Man is an Island' as a poem, yet it contains the poetic words 'Seek not to know for whom the bell tolls, it tolls for thee' and could easily be chopped up into lines and read as a free verse poem. Is the 'Song of Solomon' prose? Would John Donne's sermon be less of a piece of writing if it were chopped up?

I think that what we are talking about when we use the word poetry today is a form of writing that can beg, borrow, scavenge and steal from any other form of discourse - a railway timetable, a shopping list, a teacher's speech mannerisms, a problem in arithmetic. It can also borrow from any poetic form known to humankind - a haiku, an acrostic, a limerick, an epic, a ballad and so on. Poetry is not only a dialogue about experience between us, it is also a dialogue with all other forms and patterns of language. This has a special importance for us working in schools.

Schools are in many senses houses of instruction. Children arrive at the age of five into a place where language seems to be available mostly in certain fixed forms. For many children it is the first time that they hear that they can be 'wrong' about language, especially when they try to write it. A lot of the time in schools, language is used as a means of instruction, correction, warning and control. (As a bit of fun you could try sampling language use in schools, looking at notices, handouts, what people are saying to each other.) What poetry offers is the possibility that language can be used for entirely different purposes: to affect people through the play of language; to enable the writer, through the act of writing, to discover something about herself; to enable a community of writers, like a class, or a school, to create a shared set of understandings; to enable individuals and groups to discover in each other different and valid experiences and identities.

I have travelled some way from my criticism of the standard poetry text book for teachers with its 1. Read a poem - 2. Write a poem, but now my problem with such books should be clearer. Such a process, repeated in a mechanical way, will not provide the ground on which poetry can have the purposes and value that I have just outlined. It may, in the short term, be successful. It may provide certain satisfactions and a sense of achievement to some, possibly many, children, but, and here's the rub, after a while, I would argue, it often turns into a law of diminishing returns: the poetry that the children write begins not to *matter*.

So it occurred to me that for the teaching of poetry in schools to deepen, what was needed was not a longer, better, more varied, or cleverer book of poetry exercises, triggers or things to do. What was needed, surely, was for a group of teachers who were interested in poetry to spend a year experimenting, trying things out and talking with each other about what they are doing, and then to follow that up by writing about their experiences for other teachers to read. I put this proposal to Myra Barrs at CLPE and so, in the school year 1994 - 95, a group of teachers met three or four times a term to do just that. We read poetry, talked about poetry, shared poetry from classrooms, and wrote poetry ourselves, sometimes taking turns to run poetry workshops for the others. At the end of the year we pulled everything together into this book, and we also ran a conference at CLPE for other teachers.

Starting Points

Here is a summary of where I was coming from when we came together for the first time.

1 Every child has 'experience' and every child comes from a 'culture'.

2 Children usually express these aspects of identity orally.

3 When we initiate children into literacy, we tend to do so in a written mode. We ask children to write in shapes and patterns that many, if not most, of them do not possess. For children who do not speak standard English, this means that the business of learning how to write is an act of double translation - first, to learn how to put the things they say into writing and second, to learn how to put that writing into another dialect or language. This is difficult and inhibiting.

4 This does not always have to be the case. In poetry, children can quite legitimately express themselves in a written form that approximates much more closely to their own spoken language, whatever that might be.

5 Poetry is a way of writing that scavenges from all other language forms. It can mock or parody or adopt any kind of discourse in the air.

6 The writing of poetry does not have to be directly connected to the reading of poetry. Sometimes it is a good idea that the reading of poetry is just that, with no end product in view. Making a classroom 'poetry-

friendly' might be achieved at the outset by *not* automatically linking reading with writing.

7 Making a classroom 'poetry-friendly' can mean any of the following: reading poetry out loud to children as entertainment, just before break or going-home time; making a poetry box, a poetry corner, a poetry shelf; encouraging children to choose their own poems to read and request; enabling the children to read favourite poems on to tape, to act them out, to make poem-posters, to make their own anthologies, to make music, dance and mime triggered off by poems.

8 Making a classroom 'poetry-*writing*-friendly' can mean any of the following:

i) we can start from talk, a child's question, an anecdote from the teacher's experience, an event in the school or the class that has caused a buzz.

ii) we can home in on our lives, something scary, something funny, an argument, a situation in the home like breakfast, or being ill. We can ask of that moment some questions like: what are people saying? what am I thinking? what can I see? what can I hear? what am I saying? We can take the answers to those questions and use them to make a poem. We might want to leave it like that - a fragmented impression of a moment - or we can move the answers round, add bits, take bits away, repeat bits, make a rhythm with them. It's at moments like that, in the drafting and changing, that the experience of knowing and reading plenty of poems in a 'poetry-friendly' room will tell, as other shapes and patterns of poetry come to mind .

iii) we can make oral group poems by using a refrain like '*after dark, after dark*'. Everyone can think of something they've seen, heard, or thought '*after dark*'. The children call out one after the other, a few words each, and after every three or four children, everyone whispers '*after dark, after dark*'. The same can be done for other shared experiences like being at the swimming pool, on the bus, on the beach, being ill, or getting told off.

iv) we can make monologues, from inside someone else's head - a character from a book, from TV, or someone we know. These monologues can be internal or spoken, or can be turned into dialogues and interviews.

v) we can use any of the forms of language that the children are familiar with e.g. adverts, playground rhymes, rap, parents' speech, teachers' speech, and play with them. Raps about a neighbourhood, parents' speech on trying to get children ready for school, adverts for something unusual, like hands.

vi) poetry can be a way of preserving important memories, important moments from the past. By preserving them in writing we sort them into an order and then hold them up for reflection.

9   Poems flourish in an atmosphere of sympathetic sharing. This may be with partners in the class, parents, friends, a whole class, or the whole school. This means they can be acted out, recorded on tape, accompanied by movement and mime. They can be produced as hand-made manuscripts with decoration, drawings, cartoons, or as computer versions for reproduction as magazines and books. They can have their place in evening cultural displays in the context of dancing, storytelling and singing.

10   You know when poetry starts to matter to a child or a class when you see them reading poetry by choice, asking you to read and re-read their favourites, or when you see them choosing to write poems of their own accord and stimulated by each other.

This book, then, is a series of accounts by practising teachers of their work with children over one school year. In one very important sense these teachers differ from many, perhaps most, teachers in primary schools: they have spent a year in a group, talking to each other, keeping a journal and keeping examples of the children's writing, and finally producing accounts of what they have been up to. What they have actually done in classrooms, what they think and what they say about working with poetry, should be of great value to anyone interested in children's poetry. But perhaps there is another implied value in their experience. What they have done as a group could be reproduced anywhere, any time, by any group of teachers. We are much more than the sum of our parts. In discussion and sharing of highs and lows of experience and work in schools, we make discoveries and we develop ideas in ways that are not easily expressed on the page. I hope that this book, besides being of use for teachers in an individual way, will also encourage groups of teachers to come together and do what we did.

Michael Rosen

So you may ask yourself, how did I get here?

Ally Mullany

I'm going to begin this chapter with two snapshots of my classroom in the year of the Poetry Workshop, one from the autumn term, and the other from the following summer term.

September

We, the children and I, were still sussing each other out in those early days of a new academic year. The honeymoon period was coming to an end and we were engaged in a topic on 'Weather and the effects of the weathering'. Although it was predominately a science-based topic, I also wanted to gauge the children's interest and confidence with poetry. In whole class discussions and during individual reading discussions I had already been getting some idea of the children's feelings about reading and writing poetry. The overall feeling seemed to be 'It's O.K. I suppose'. No child said 'I really like this poem' or 'I remember that one'. In three or four Primary Language Record conferences, children had specifically said 'I don't like poetry'; in general children did not appear to have had significant access to reading poetry. In the classroom, resources of poetry books were very limited. As for writing poetry, when I introduced a task there were distinct groans and fidgets.

Prior to writing ourselves, we read aloud some poetry with a weather theme. Some poems were chosen by me and some by children who had been asked to see what they could find. We also talked about different associations for specific types of weather. All rather predictable stuff really.

Eight children who lacked confidence with their writing worked with the primary helper. They journeyed out to the playground on what was a reasonably windy autumnal day to do some 'jottings'. They talked about what they saw and felt and recorded, either personally or with the primary helper, some of the words and feelings that sprang to mind as they 'faced the wind; watched the trees; looked at the buildings; touched stones/brick' etc. Returning to the classroom, they stayed with the primary helper to work on their compositions.

The rest of the class worked individually. Some chose to read for themselves some of the poems I had read or went on to find other poems before actually starting to write. I emphasised the importance of getting your ideas down rather than worrying about transcription.

The outcome of all this was that all children presented their initial drafts in prose. A few had experimented with repetition. The overall feeling in the class was 'Finished, miss, what do I do now?'. Not a great deal of enthusiasm, to say the least.

To get the children to review the visual presentation of their work we looked at different ways poems had been printed in books. Second drafts looked different. Some children had seen some shape poems and so rewrote their poems in this style, which became popular. We had snowmen, raindrops, tornadoes, suns, a meteorologist's nightmare - however, there was a spark of commitment now to the task. With one exception none of the children changed or felt the need to adjust their composition.

The overall outcome went on display in the classroom. The children were satisfied with their work but I felt I had a serious 'selling' task on my hands to engender a sense of enjoyment and pleasure in reading and writing and poetry. In particular I wanted the children to develop an independent and unique feel to their work.

April

It's the first week of the summer term. Next week there is a whole school celebration of books, with authors and illustrators visiting, a daily book fair, and a school poetry competition. I announce all this.

'Great'. 'Wicked'. 'Is Michael Rosen coming?' 'Is the person who wrote *Talking Turkeys* coming?' In response to news of the poetry competition, whoops of delight and 'Can I do one about . . .?' When calmness was restored, and with real commitment, this is how we kicked off.

I was keen for the children to write a poem that was personally inspired and not teacher or topic driven. I was aware of the possibility that, given an open palette, there would be a feeling of 'What shall I write about?' or several cases of writer's block. To offset this we set about creating a 'menu' for ourselves. I read some of my favourite poems to the whole class and asked the children to volunteer to read some of their favourites. In doing this we came up with some word

patterns. Poems that started with, or repeated phrases such as:

'When I...', 'If I were...', 'What is...', 'I looked...', 'If I had...' (this last phrase was taken from a song I had introduced to the class in a mathematics money topic - *If I had a million dollars* by Bare Naked Ladies, a Canadian group). We also identified popular poem types such as animal poems, picture/shape poems, acrostic poems.

Finally, I introduced into our menu some art pictures, and asked children to suggest a title for the paintings. They were the *Mona Lisa*, *The Road*, and Hiroshige's *Mount Fuji*. The first two generated the most discussion and we arrived at the following titles for poems. 'Where does the road go?'

I recorded the children's ideas for the menu as our discussion developed and we ended up with twelve options. The children were asked to choose one they felt comfortable with or else suggest a good alternative prior to leaving the whole class group to compose their individual poems. Those children choosing the painting-inspired option took a copy of the painting with them. None of the children had any difficulty in 'getting going', although some, particularly those who opted for the acrostic format, changed their option following their early attempts. I think this option initially served to build an element of confidence in writing, as it was a format that the children felt comfortable with and would often dabble with. But after their acrostic attempts, their writing developed in different directions.

Initial drafts flowed quickly, there was an air of enjoyment and children went on to read their poems to each other in groups. They asked me to listen to or read their poems, and then moved on to change elements of their compositions or to write another poem. Following the two sessions, and on completion of our 'best copies' for the competition, there were requests to do it all again.

Pictures and poems

The poem which went on to win a prize in the competition was written by a boy who previously only wrote raps. As it was a competition I had encouraged the children to attempt a different form of poetry from anything they had done previously, in order to surprise the judges! This writer was not keen at first, but through gentle ego-boosting he eventually said 'I'll try'. He sat very quietly at a table, looking at the picture for some time. I visited him on a couple of occasions and 're-boosted' him. I was just about to give in and suggest he write a rap, when he started to write.

The poem came out complete, virtually on first draft. There were a few minor spelling errors. He and I were both stunned!

The lady with the secret smile

She looks like dark thunder,
strikes so
bright, the wind passes by and
blows
the leaves off the trees.

She looks like a dark swan that
swoops in at night when no one
ever
sees it here at night

She looks like a cat which purrs
and
kills the birds and fish

Her smile goes round the
corridors
She stares at me like thunder,
strikes like the wind.

One day her eyes were looking
the other way, mysterious
MONA.

by Leon

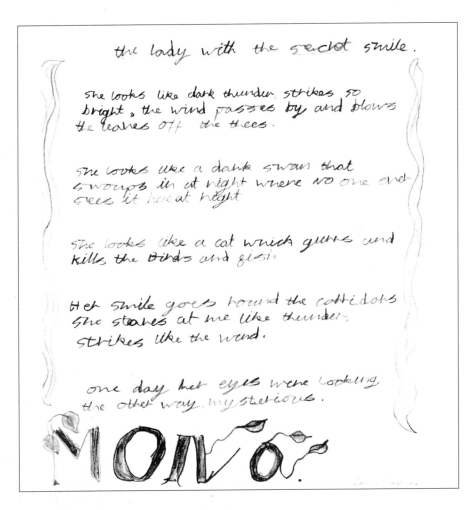

Another entrant to the competition wrote about a different picture:

Where does the road go?

Where does the road go?
Over the sea?
Where pearls sparkle?

Over the bridges?
Where people walk
With four and two legs go

In the rivers
Where the sticklebacks swim

In the sewers
Where rats and
Beetles and flies
Walk and fly.

In the sky
Where butterflies
and birds fly.

by Christopher

still had a prose format, which some changed spontaneously, and others with the help of more direct teacher intervention. My interventions were largely based on how the child read the poem aloud. I would suggest that where they changed their intonation they could find a way of signalling their intentions to the reader through (for instance) line breaks.

War poems

This pattern of working filtered through to another task when we were studying the Blitz and its impact on the local area. Children had interviewed people who were there. They also had visual evidence of the effects of war (photographs, artists' responses). In their poems, some used repetition in an entirely appropriate way:

War Poem

The bombs are coming!
The bombs are coming!
run! run! run!
get your gas mask!
get your gas mask!
run! run! run!
People are dying!
People are dying!
aeroplanes are coming!
aeroplanes are coming!
run! run! run!
get the light out!
get the light out!
Quick! quick! quick!

by Tony

So you may ask yourself, how did I get here?

The words of that song seem appropriate. When I compared these two sequences of work with the same children, I wondered how their opinions and the quality of their work could have changed so dramatically. In reviewing my teaching year and the developing interest, involvement and enthusiasm about poetry shown by this group of Year 4 children, I considered the different ways we had explored and experimented with poetry.

I started with a personal love of poetry, in which I myself have been a late developer. From the beginning I knew that I did not want to influence children too much towards a particular style of poetry. My aim throughout has been to engender reading and writing poetry for pleasure. We would regularly use poetry as a form of relaxation and something to treat ourselves with.

We boosted the availability of poetry books in the classroom through loans from the local education authority library and through teachers' personal resources. These included tapes of poetry with accompanying texts.

In the first term we used our story time of half an hour at the end of each day to explore and indulge ourselves with poetry. These times started with me choosing poems of different kinds and reading them to the class, but after a few sessions the children began to recommend poems, which I then encouraged them to read to the class. The emphasis was specifically on enjoying listening and reading rather than on any writing. Children started to visit the school library to look for poetry and some brought in books from home. As a class we started to adopt some favourite poets. Hot favourites were Brian Patten, Michael Rosen, Roald Dahl, Judith Nicholls and Kit Wright.

In response to a whole school focus on 'Me and My Family' we had another go at writing poetry, using Brian Patten's *The Trouble with My Sister*, *The Trouble with My Brother*, for inspiration. The children enjoyed the humour of these poems and were interested in their own compositions. Initial drafts

The trouble with war

The trouble with war is they never
get play time.
The trouble with war is there's
too much noise.
The trouble with war is you don't
stay alive.
The trouble with war is there's
not enough people.
The trouble with war is you don't
get a chance to play.
The trouble with war is turn off
your lights.
The trouble with war is you never
know if your house is there.
The trouble with war is you never
get a chance to sleep.
The trouble with war is when the
full moon comes out you never
come out from your house.

A connection between the sound and
rhythm of a poem and its subject
seemed to be developing.

Responding to music

Throughout the year we had a
particular focus on classical music. We
explored each new piece through
dance, movement and poetry. These
were not necessarily consecutive
sessions, and children were often
working on interpretations at different
times and in different contexts. The
following poem arose out of a study of
Greig's *The Hall of the Mountain King*:

The Troll King

I'm a really powerful King
I really really like being who I am.
I like being ugly and dirty.
I tell people what to do.
I like not working, just relaxing
indoors.
I scare all of my slaves and I
whip them.
I like that, I really really like that.
I hate all of my slaves, they stink
bad.
I have blue hairs all over me, I
like it.
I like being smelly.
I have loads of cooks
I have four arms, three legs
I'm a really really nasty troll.

by Katie

Spontaneous poetry

Often children would write about things that happened in a kind of diary fashion. Poetry started to be an attractive avenue for those children who did not have much confidence in literacy or for whom English was a second language. I was particularly touched by this poem as it was written by a boy who had specifically said 'I don't like poetry' earlier in the year. He wrote it at home:

My Day Out

I went out
with my friend
we played football
it was good
on the grass
My friend said
let's play He
We did it was
good as well
I like it I said
I bring my dog out
it caught my friend
it got my finger it
bit my finger
he went to
hospital two weeks
he was better we
played out side
again and my dog
didn't bite again.

by Adel

Often we would plan poetry sessions into a topic but poetry also became something to do when the children felt they had finished tasks. This example was in response to another curriculum topic. It's written, obviously from inside the Trojan Horse!:

Odysseus

Come on mates
we can do it
I'll shine the torch, yea!
I will get out first.
You will follow. Let's get out now!
Remember what I said.
They're coming now.
Hi, mates,
I'll fight Paris.
Menelaus, you get the lady.
Soldiers and princes and kings,
you fight their army.
Then we will set fire to their palace
we will stay there till we win,
then we leave.

by Katie

A group of eight children had been targetted in the Spring term for specific reading support. Some supply cover was available and I also had a student during this term. They were children who needed a boost to improve their reading and understanding of English. Poetry was our means to this. It enabled experimentation with reading-aloud styles and stimulated play with words. The games played in some of these sessions were taken back to the rest of the group and children were often heard at reading times experimenting with reading in different voices and with different intonations.

'I'm here and I'm ready to write'

Finally, a comment made by one of the more 'reluctant' workers in the class during the final days of term, in response to an invitation to write poetry. 'I'm here and I'm ready to write', he said. This surprising remark was more evidence of the change that had taken place in this group of children. The approach I used during the year was not a hard and fast one, but it seemed to work for them. If I was asked to say what it involved, I'd include: recognising that poetry is different, celebrating it as a unique element in the curriculum, not treating it with 'kid gloves', allowing children to experiment.

In the course of the year, as children progressed in confidence and self-esteem, we celebrated their compositions through displays,

through whole class sharing, through reading aloud, through creating books of their compositions. The presence of a real poet during our book week was certainly an incentive - but the use of video can bring the poets out of the books too.

So where do I go now? - I shall need to start 'selling' poetry all over again in the new term, when I plan to take an infants class. It will be important for me to remember that it might take time and a lot of 'selling' to free up the children and make them feel

comfortable with poetry. You need commitment and stamina, and it helps to have termly objectives to keep you on track. But although planning is important, I think one of the things I have learnt from this year is not to expect a set outcome from an activity, but rather to ensure that every child is encouraged to participate. The chance of being surprised rises enormously as a consequence.

Ally Mullany
formerly of Rotherhithe Primary School

Juicy Bits: developing a taste for poetry

Andrew Lambirth

My objective for the workshop year was to encourage children to begin to write poetry that would be meaningful to them, and to use poetry to express themselves in some way. I wanted them to feel relaxed and at home with the medium, and I wanted to hear an authentic child's voice in their work.

I was working with a class of year 5, nine- and ten-year olds that I had assumed would have been asked to write poetry previously in their school life. The children knew how to recognise poetry on a page, and all had their favourites, but when asked to write themselves there was a general reluctance to have a go. Their completed work reflected a confusion in their minds about how to write a poem, and about what a good one would look like.

Before discussing our actual poetry writing sessions, I think it is important to examine the background poetry activity which went on all through the year in the classroom, a backdrop which certainly influenced children's attitudes and motivation. Our class reading area had a small box stuffed with a variety of poetry texts which were popular with the class. Children of all reading abilities seemed interested in reading poetry. We would regularly end our reading times by children reading what I called 'Juicy Bits' from the books they had been looking at. It was often here that children chose to read poetry. Tony Bradman's collections were popular, and so were poems about certain subjects like food or ghosts. *Please Mrs Butler* was well loved, and Michael Rosen's books, such as *The Hypnotiser,* were well read. As well as the children reading poetry I would also choose to read a poem to the class myself before lunch each day.

This was some of the ground work, but how was I actually going to start encouraging these children to become poets? *Language Matters,* the journal of the Centre for Language in Primary Education, had just run an article about getting started with children writing poetry. The writers of the article helpfully suggested reading poetry with a certain structure to the class and asking children to use this structure in their poems. One poem they mentioned was Wes Magee's *What is the Sun* from his book *The Witch's Brew.* Here the children needed to think up lots of metaphors to describe the sun. It worked! My class wrote some pleasing poems in response to this poem.

I did feel, however, that although the children had responded well to this exercise, had completed the task, and were even pleased with the results, we had still not moved on far along the road to writing authentic children's poetry. It reminded me of occasions when I have seen water colour paintings produced by children under the heavy direction of an adult. This direction would always be technique-driven. Initially one can be knocked out by how like 'real' adult water colour paintings these children's productions are, until you realise that they all look identical; they have been churned out in the same way because all the children have followed the same mechanical process. The 'technique' is actually hiding any authentic talent that may be there.

What next? I tried to find a poem with a clear structure that children had found interesting enough to read and discuss themselves. I was still pursuing the idea that providing this kind of scaffolding would raise the confidence of the class for writing poetry. Brian Patten's *Feeding the Family* was the piece I chose. This was well known and well liked. The poem describes how members of the family are fed disgusting things and how they react. The children enjoyed writing their own versions of this poem. It stimulated them to write with enthusiasm, using their own day-to-day sense of humour for a legitimate school purpose. Because of this, there were authentic children's voices appearing in these pieces. It was, however, still very much a school exercise.

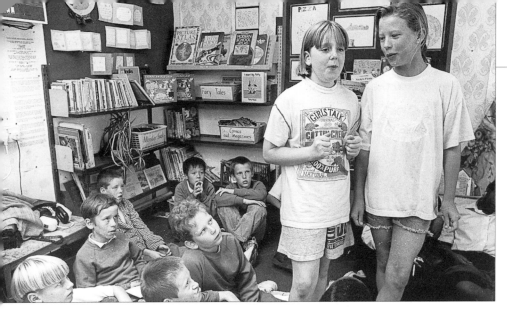

Dramatising poems

Meanwhile the background activity was still going on. My class performed an assembly in which they dramatised poems that I had found for them. We used three poems: *Superstink* by Robert Froman, *All for an Ice Cream* by Karen Jackson and *Yellow Butter* by Mary Ann Hoberman. In preparation for this performance the children were asked to get into groups, share the lines out and make what they would of the poem. The results of this were extremely good. The children brought in their own props and costumes and took the whole thing much further than I had imagined. We had great acting, which brought the poems to life and extended the boundaries of the children's understanding of how you can perform a poem.

Food poems

Back to the writing and now it was breakthrough time for my Rotherhithe poets. Food is a subject which is always on children's lips, so to speak, and I thought I would stick with this subject. Once again I read to the class a certain poem which I hoped would provide a stimulus for their own work. I chose Frank Flynn's *Spaghetti*. This time I was using a poem not for its structure, but for its theme, its idea; it is a poem with a strong serious side that children recognised. Yes, it's a poem about eating squiggly spaghetti, but it is also about the love of food and the private and personal way we choose to eat food. My class tuned into this idea very quickly, and we had an important discussion about the food they liked and particularly about how and where they liked to eat it.

It was this angle that provided the most stimulation for their writing and was the reason that I was subsequently given such delightful and personal poems. The discussion revealed that nearly everyone ate certain foods in an individual or peculiar way. We had children who broke open sandwich biscuits and would scrape off the inside and discard the rest. We even had one child who described how he enjoyed eating a Big Mac while at the same time sucking cola up through a straw in his nose. (He wanted to call his poem *My mum says I've got a disgusting habit*). But most were just personal observations which described how serious and private an activity eating can be for a child of nine or ten.

Corinne's poem is a good example:

Sunday Dinner
Chicken, Potatoes and Carrots

I like my Sunday Dinner because sometimes I eat it in peace.

Sometimes when I eat it in peace my dog starts to bark

But there you go.

Sometimes when I eat the meat, the actual meat on the bone

I say to myself "That was lovely"

Then I start sucking the bone dry.

then I go on to the other one and do the same with that one.

Then I go on to the potatoes

They are lovely and crispy, the inside is hot and I can see the

Steam coming out.

Then I eat my carrots, they are lovely but not as nice as the

Meat and the potatoes.

It was interesting that some children still made reference to the original poem by Frank Flynn, as in Hung Vi's poem:

Pizza

I love pizza.

It looks like a triangle with circles and ham on.

I take off the pepperami and throw it in my mouth.

I take off all the cheese and slosh it in my mouth

And some of the pieces fall on my shirt.

I go to the mirror

I've got tomato sauce . . . and I wipe it on my sister!

by Hung Vi

I would like to stress here how many of the children took their ideas from the discussion that was held after the reading of the poem. This was without a doubt the strongest influence on and motivation for their work. The poem had provided the initial idea, but our talk together made them expand the concept and generate their own ideas. At the point when they went off to start their composition they were brimming with thoughts of what they were going to write. Had I just asked them to go off and write about their favourite food, I know I would not have had the success I had with them that day. It

was tuning in to something personal that they all recognised in themselves and in each other which made their pieces original.

Writing about something they knew, I now recognised to be very important, but almost equally important was their having models to compare their work with. Hearing poetry regularly, reading and performing it, must take equal precedence with writing poetry. Since reading and performing poems which were based on dialogue, the children accepted this way of writing as poetry, as in *All for an Ice Cream*, for example.

Dialogue poems

On one particular occasion, a discussion from a book slowly turned into a period of poetry writing. I had just read *Up in the Stars* by Dyan Sheldon and we started to discuss what it was like to be bored at home. The children started reporting what their parents said when they announced that they were bored. Some hilarious dialogues between mother or father and child were coming out, and we suddenly started to realise how like *All For an Ice Cream* our stories were. Their narration of events seemed clearly influenced by this type of dialogue-rich poetry.

When I said 'That would make good poetry', this influenced the stories even more. So we went away and wrote, and individuals read their poems out during the writing period. Here are some examples. It's interesting to note how, as well as the influence of Karen Jackson's poem, the children gave each other ideas:

I'm Bored

"Muuuuuuummy I love you"
"What do you want?"
"I'm bored Muuuuuummy"
"Well go and tidy your room then"
"I've done that already Muuuuuummy"
"Go out and play then"
"I've got no one to play with Muuuuuummy"
"Why don't you do some times tables then"
"Did I say that I love you Muuuuuummy?"
"Twelves or nines"
"I'm not bored now Mum"

by Victoria

I am Bored

"Mummy I am bored"

"Go and clean your room then"

"But I've already done that it Mummy"

"Well go and clean my room then"

"Oh but Mummy that's your room though Mummy"

"Go and play with your games or play on the computer"

"Okay Mummy".

Ten minutes later

"Mummy I'm bored, I've got nothing to do Mummy"

"Look will you stop moaning at me, I've got my own things to do you know"

"But Mummy I'm bored though"

"Go out and play or something I've got my tests coming up you know"

"Oh Mummy I've got no one to play with though"

"Look if you don't stop moaning I'll send you up to your room, or maybe a maths test would cheer you up"

"Er Mummy I'll think I'll clean my room instead, have a nice day bye"

by Wen Zhiao

I'm Bored

"Mum"

"What"

"I'm bored"

"Why don't you play on your computer"

"No"

"Why?"

"That's boring"

"Go out and play football"

"No"

"Why?"

"Cos we've just been playing football, and it's boring"

"Well, go and clean the toilet, then tidy your room then . . ."

"I'll play on my computer"

"I thought it was boring"

"It bloody ain't now!"

"Get to your room!"

"Arrrr Mummmmmmm"

"NOW"

"IT AIN'T FAIR"

by Stephen

These two last examples, the 'private' food poems and the dialogue poetry, illustrate two of the most important ingredients in attempting to encourage children to have a go at poetry writing, perhaps summed up by one word - experience. By this I mean both experience of a wide range of poetry by different writers *and* tuning into the experiences and concerns of children of the age you are working with. This way you get to hear the authentic voices of children writing about things they truly understand, in a way which reflects their understanding of what a poem can be.

Without that confident understanding, nourished by constant exposure to an eclectic selection of poetry texts, they would not have been able to take up the invitation to write. Without discussion, the opportunity to talk over subjects that they know well and come to understand some of the subtleties and intricacies of them, they would not have been able to fuel each other's ideas for poetry. Real feelings, known experience, turned into poetry.

Andrew Lambirth
formerly of Rotherhithe Primary School
London Borough of Southwark

Two children

Colette Morris

During the months that I have been focusing on poetry in my Year 2 classroom the question that has gained more and more importance for me is: what makes this child want to write poetry? This question emerged during the first two months of the year, when the children were introduced to various poets and poems. Although they were prepared to write, and copied techniques competently, there seemed to be no connection between poetry and themselves. I began to ask myself: Why am I doing this? Where are they going with it? What do I want them to be doing?

I felt that in order to be able to study poetry in any depth when they were older, children needed to experience it as a product of their own voice. I was not so much interested in them being able to use any particular form as in them finding any way of voicing their own experience, about their friends, their parents, their loves, their hates, their God.

When I came to choose my particular focus, I decided to try to answer my own question in relation to two children, who I felt both needed a voice for different reasons.

Ayo

Ayo (smiling broadly) said that poetry was 'rubbish', which for him was a way of saying 'I can't make sense of that'. I needed to win him over because he was so vocal that his opinions were always reflected in the rest of the class. If Ayo said so, then it was!

Ayo was an enthusiastic reader who loved to read out loud to everyone, and to hear things read. When I read aloud to the class *Nuts about Nuts* and *Come On into My Tropical Garden*, he was very vocal indeed about his objections to both of them. But in November I noticed he had started going to to the poetry shelf and reading quietly. He also chose a poetry book when we visited the library - *Poems Not to Be Missed* - although he went to great lengths not to let anyone see it.

Although Ayo would talk about anything and had a great sense of humour, his confidence in speaking was not reflected in his writing, and he did not enjoy writing. During this time I made the decision to scribe for him during poetry sessions. I was unsure about whether I should do this because Ayo actually could write, but was just not sufficiently confident to put his ideas down on paper. But I only had to scribe for him twice. Both times, when I asked him to read it aloud, the other children laughed and clapped.

Although Ayo was now happier to write (perhaps because he wanted to read his poems aloud!), he seemed to find it easier if he had a structure. One he began to use a lot was from a game we played in drama, 'opposites'. He had carried this game through into class talk and thought it was fun to talk in opposites. After hearing *I Don't Like the Dark* on the radio programme 'Poetry Corner', Ayo used opposites to write this poem:

The Dark

I like the dark because you can watch T.V.

I like the dark because it is fun.

I like the dark because you can watch scary films

I like the dark.

I don't like the dark because it is not fun

I don't like the dark because if you watch the Nightmare before Christmas

you may get bad dreams

I don't like the dark.

Again I asked Ayo to read his poem aloud and it was received with nods of approval.

Over the following months Ayo decided that he did like poetry. He brought in poems for me to read and he began to read to himself the poems that I read aloud. In February an author and storyteller, Margaret Bateson-Hill, visited the school to tell her story *Lao Lao of Dragon Mountain*. After that, the children had been living and breathing dragons. We had also read *Lend Me Your Wings* by John Agard and *Tigerella* by Kit Wright.

One day I was reading Tigerella again, and talking to the children about stories that were written as poems, when Ayo said: 'I did that'. 'When?' I asked. 'For my story, my dragon story', he said. The children work on the stories they want to make into books and Ayo had been drafting a story. I asked him to fetch it and read it. This is what he read:

A big dragon in my house

There is a dragon in my house
he is big and scary

He flies around my house all night

and doesn't let us sleep at all.

There is a dragon in my house

He is not only scary he is very very greedy

and he always eats my food.

There's a dragon in my kitchen

He ate my mum he ate my dad
and he ate my little brother

but he didn't eat me because
he is not scary.

He doesn't eat my food and he
didn't eat my mum and my dad
and my little brother.

There is no dragon in my house

there is no dragon anywhere!

I was staggered, and the rest of the class thought it was wonderful. The poem even had performance instructions: 'loud' and 'quiet' written next to the verses. I sent Ayo immediately to read it to other classes and arranged for him to read it at assembly. He made the poem into a book and was very proud of it.

Choosing to write

By March Ayo thought of himself as a poet. He was also trying other ways of writing and he had departed from the opposites game. On Mothers' Day he tried a rap, influenced by Grace Nichols' *Baby K*. He was beginning to repeat lines and re-arrange words on the page. At about this time he listened to a poem *In the Middle of the Night* , which was brought into school by Whitney. We talked about the things we did in the middle of the night and the children went off to write. Ayo drafted this poem with no hesitation - and none of the uncertainty he had shown before:

In the Middle of the Night

In the middle of the night

I go downstairs and get some food

In the middle of the night

I go downstairs and get some food

But the cat scared me so I went back to bed

In the middle of the night

I went back downstairs

and this time the dog appeared

so I hit the cat and hit the dog

and went back to bed

in the middle of the night.

Ayo looks at how a poem is written now. He still enjoys repeating lines because he is confident that he can use that format to say what he wants. Writing about birds, after having read some of the bird poems in *Hist Whist* by ee cummings, Ayo wrote:

Pigeons Pigeons Pigeons

everyone tries to catch them

pigeons pigeons pigeons

they are very fat

when I throw bread for the little birds

the fat pigeons take them away

pigeons pigeons pigeons

everyone tries to catch them

pigeons pigeons pigeons

they are very fat.

Ayo often chooses to write poetry. He also tells me about new poetry books he has seen or that his mother has bought him. His latest is the new Brian Patten book he saw on the television. When I asked Ayo to write something for me about poetry he wrote:
'I forgot why I didn't like poems before but I know why I like it now and I am going to tell you. I like it now because I like all the rhyming words because they are funny. My best poem is *Don't Do* by Michael Rosen.'

Ayo seemed to have come full circle. The poem he started off disliking is now at the top of his list!

Whitney

Whitney was a very quiet and reflective child who worked hard and said very little. She rarely spoke unless she was addressed directly, and quite easily disappeared in class discussion. She enjoyed reading, but would never volunteer to read aloud. She also loved to write, but wrote far more for herself at home than she ever wrote in school. I felt that she needed a voice and realised that it was particularly important to encourage her to be more vocal because, when she did participate, she inspired others. Whitney was confident within her female peer group, and this was the group on which she drew for support.

In the course of the autumn term, I began to notice that Whitney was putting little poems on the home board, poems that reflected what we were doing in class. I started to ask her to read them aloud and the more I asked her, the more she wrote and the more she brought in.

In November we had listened to 'Poetry Corner' and Whitney had been inspired to write a poem called *Yummy Yummy*. I asked her to read it aloud. The next day the first part of the poem appeared on the home board, so I asked her to read it again:

Yummy Yummy bread and butter

in my tummy bread is nice

to lick and it is so thick

and it nice to

spice like tins of rice

Rice is nice to dish with fish

to eat with meat have one

with ham honey and jam

I like icecream it soft

and cold it nice to lick

and hold on a stick

It's nice to mix and

mash it up

icecream in a cup

icecream I eat it all up.

I like cake to dish and

bake to eat all up to

take a break.

Whitney was enjoying using rhyming words but the poem was also an explanation of how she felt. In November she wrote, in response to a poem on *Poetry Corner*:

I don't like the day because you

can hear strange noise and it makes

me scared when I watch a scary film.

I have nightmares at night that's why

I don't like the night but I do

like the light.

For Ayo this theme had been an opportunity to play with opposites; for Whitney it was a chance to tell people how she felt about the dark. She read it aloud and we used 'carpet time' to discuss what different styles of poetry people were using and which authors they had got their ideas from.

Asking questions

To help children start looking at how to structure poems we sometimes used the 'asking questions' technique that Michael Rosen had introduced to the CLPE poetry workshop group:

What are you doing?

What is someone else doing?

What is someone else saying?

What are you thinking?

We used variations of these questions depending on what we were doing. In January we visited the Unicorn Theatre to watch *Aladdin*. Whitney used this question method for her poem:

A genie came to visit me

he asked me what my wish
would be

I looked I stared I got scared

I jumped into the air he pulled
my hair

It look like me probably

what did it say? I grant your
wish today

What did you think? It kept
making me blink.

Whitney had continued to use the home board and the genie poem appeared the day after the theatre visit. I asked her to read it aloud. After this Whitney began to hand me her poems and discuss them before putting them on the board.

In February, after the visit from the storyteller, Whitney brought in her *Oxford Dragon* poetry book and I asked her to read her favourite poem aloud. By this time Whitney was reading aloud really confidently and I told her that if there was any other poetry she had written that she would like to share, she could bring it in. She brought in a poem she had written for her aunt going away:

When
there are fears
I know there be tears
when you are sad
I won't get mad
when you go on
a trip and make
a start I know
I'll always be
in your heart.

Whitney wrote directions for performance of her poem:
'We stand in a half circle and at the end when I say "Go on a trip and make a start I know I always be in your

heart" we can make a plane and pretend someone's going on a plane.'

Ayo suggested she read the poem in assembly when he read his. Whitney agreed. I was surprised that she had enough confidence to do that. She read loudly and clearly.
In March we had been looking at the use of repeating lines and Whitney had brought in her Oxford poetry books. I asked her to choose one she wanted to read and she chose *In the Middle of the Night*. In the session that followed, Whitney wrote:

In the middle of the night
While everything was quiet
A rat crept in to my room
And sat on my hat

In the middle of the night
While I slept
the rat touched my arm
and I screamed
with a fright
in the middle
of the night.

A playground rap

A friend of Whitney's in class had brought in *Lend Me your Wings* by John Agard. We read it in class and talked about his use of language. I also showed them *No Hickory No Dickory No Dock* and *Say It Again Granny*. We were then plunged into SATs. I found that instead of writing poetry in the classroom, Whitney and her friend (Whitney was by now considered to be the expert) had transferred their poetry making to the playground. They had really enjoyed *Baby K* by Grace Nichols and they started to create their own rap, bringing in each part as they wrote it and putting it on the home board:

> Keep our world
> nice and clean that's
> de golden rule
>
> Get in a circle eat
> your thing then
> throw your rubbish
> in the bin
> that's how we keep our world
> nice and clean.
>
> You shouldn't throw your
> rubbish on the floor
> do you know why
> it's against the Law.
>
> Keep our world
> spick and span
> Don't throw your
> ham wraps
> on the ground.

> (Chorus)
> You got to throw your
> rubbish in the bin and
> keep our world
> nice and clean.
>
> You got to
> share cars and give
> good air
> so people can survive
> that's Fair.
>
> You got to give air
> for sufferers of asthma
> like me
> and my friends
> (Chorus)

The children decided they wanted to use this rap in the end of term concert and we set about rehearsing it. Whitney wanted to perform part of it, and she also wanted to include *Baby K* in the performance. Finally Whitney and her friends persuaded Zoe to perform the *Baby K* rap in the concert. Zoe had learnt the whole thing off by heart because she loved it so and she stunned us all by performing it brilliantly in class one day. I have a feeling she could have performed the whole book.

So the concert performance consisted of their own rap, John Agard's rap and some dialogues worked out by Ayo and some friends for arguing about pollution, using *Tuba This Tuba That* from *Kiskadee Queen* by Faustin Charles.

The self-confidence that Whitney had gained through poetry meant that she was now able to help organise and structure our performance. Whitney's mum was really proud of her. 'I didn't think she'd have the confidence' she said. All the parents enjoyed the concert and commented on the confidence of the children.

Whitney decided to make a compilation of poems she had written and really enjoyed. She made a collection for the home board. She also wrote an explanation of why she enjoyed poetry, and she started to collect other people's opinions, again for the home board. Her own views were as follows:

'I like poems because I like rhyming words and I want to be a poem writer when I grow up.
I write poems because they're fun to read and I get use to them and I listen to them and I learn them.
Poems help me because they're fun. I enjoy reading them loud because I'm quiet.'

Both Ayo and Whitney had found their 'particular' voice and both had become keen writers. Although I have only written about these two children, many others became avid readers and writers of poetry during the year and this love united them as a class. They now had a shared appreciation of poetry, which started them on a journey towards the kind of deeper poetic experience that I had wanted for them at the start.

Colette Morris
formerly of English Martyrs Primary School
London Borough of Southwark

25

A Poetry Journal: a year with Year 6

Varina Emblen

September

We had a general discussion amongst the class as to what poetry is, or what it isn't. After much discussion and several examples, we still could not really agree on a common formula and decided that a poem could take any format, could have any amount of - or no - punctuation, could rhyme or not, and could have rhythm or not. It was generally agreed that it was a good way of expressing feelings using only a few words - and that it was easier than writing a story!

The children then went on to choose particular poems and explain why they enjoyed them. They chose a varied selection: *Hairy Tales and Nursery Crimes* - because the humour of word play was appreciated by this Year 6 class; *Pillow Talk* - also for its humour; *Ghost Poems* - the boy who chose this said that a lot of the poems in the class were too difficult for him, but that he liked these poems because they were easy to read. They had a predictable rhythm and rhyme, so he stood a good chance of reading them correctly.

We went on to do some work on alliteration. This was linked to Raymond Briggs' *Fungus the Bogeyman* and took the form of a 'Bogey Dictionary'. For some it was a useful exercise in finding their way around a thesaurus and dictionary . Many children picked up on the idea well, but many needed more practice.

With this in mind, on another day we went on to the Sandy Brownjohn alliteration exercise - 'One wobbly waitress . . . .Two turgid tape worms,' and so on. This was more successful and enabled the children to explore with each other the tongue twisting combinations. Some of the results were surreal. After these experiences, children tackled the 'Bogey Dictionary' with more enthusiasm.

Alliteration Poem

One wicked watch waltzed
weirdly west.

Two tickly tramps twirled
towards Turkey.

Three thin thieves thumped
things

Four funny fish fought with
freckles

Five fabulous faggots had a
false fancy

Six silly salmon said
sarcastically 'shame'

Seven sausage satsumas
played a salty saxophone

Eight educated elephants eat
electric eels

Nine narrow newsagents
nibbled noisy nomads

Ten traffic trainers trained
trapeze tradesmen.

by Harriet

Alliteration Poem

One wise wolf wondered when winter would wither,

Two tiny tadpoles tried tasting a turkey,

Three fat frogs flattened a fish

Four fairies flyed through a fortress

Five firemen floating on a flounder

Six sinister swindlers stealing

Seven silly snakes slithering slowly southwards

Eight elephants eating enormous easter eggs

Nine nitwits nowhere near Norway

Ten tiny tigers trying to talk.

by Mohammed

November

After reading the article *Introducing poetry* by Helen Rosenthal (*Language Matters*, 93/94 no.2) I got interested in the idea of giving children a very definite structure or pattern to their poems. Rather than leaving them to it, the idea of following a set 'formula' seemed to be a good starting point for this lively Y6 class, and a way of enabling all the children to have a go. We began by reading *What is . . . the sun?* by Wes Magee and discussed the way the poem was written on the page. We talked about stanzas, beginnings and the fact that the poem did not rhyme. I asked the children to think about images of the sun and to link it to other objects, such as Wes Magee does in his poem. Some ideas were 'a bowl of cereal on a blue tablecloth', 'a golden stud in a velvet jewellery box', 'a red boat on a blue lagoon'.

Once they had got the idea and decided on a form that the poem should take, they hurriedly wrote their first draft in their general work books. Then they redrafted, in discussion with me, trying to use each word only once if possible. They were confident in their use of the thesaurus and dictionaries. They wrote a second draft in their language books, concentrating more on use of vocabulary and images. When they were happy with their poems they went on to write them out on decorated paper.

I thought this approach was very useful at the beginning of poetry writing with this class because:
• Having the structure given to them in this way helped everyone to write.
• It was a relatively short activity which allowed for easy redrafting, editing etc. - and which followed on from previous thesaurus/dictionary work.
• It gave many children success, and therefore developed their enthusiasm for poetry writing. They were not afraid to tackle this task and very much enjoyed the end results which we read to each other at the end of the session. We then went on to look at Grace Nichols' poem *The Sun* which the children also enjoyed.

Some of the poems they wrote:

> The sun is an orange bubble floating in the air.
>
> It is a hot balloon drifting over the calm Caribbean sea.
>
> The sun is a steaming ball shining on the Earth.
>
> It is like a corn pop floating in the air.

by Ahmed

> The sun is an amber button on a silk blue shirt.
>
> It is a shining drawing pin against a blue notice board.
>
> The sun is a glistening yellow feathered bird flying across the breezy sky.
>
> It is a light house beacon shining across the sea.
>
> It is a golden stud against a piece of smooth velvet.

by Naureen

The Sun

The sun is a golden plate on blue satin,

It is a red sauce in a blue bowl,

The sun is a yellow bed in a blue room,

It is a shining star in a daytime sky,

The sun is a red boat in a blue lagoon,

It is an orange bush in a blue forest,

The sun is a glistening coin in a blue purse,

It is the sun, it is the beautiful sun.

by Erin

December

Following a school journey in which a river study had taken place, we decided that, rather than write an account of the day, we would choose one moment from the day and write about it - either as an intensive short piece of writing or as a poem. I wanted the children to crystallise one particular moment in time when they had experienced an intense feeling. I expected them to write about the mud, falling in the water, or water over the tops of their wellies.

The lesson plan was:

- A whole group discussion about the snapshot of time; the need to ignore such details as: 'I walked along the path', 'I said to my friend "Isn't this good"' and so on. I wanted them to focus on intense, direct experiences of joy, fear, surprise etc.

- I encouraged as many of the class to contribute to the discussion as possible. Then I let them write freely for ten minutes in silence, and I wrote also.

- We went back to the beginning and decided whether we wanted to write a piece of intensive prose or a poem. The class unanimously wanted a poem. With this in mind, they 'frisked' their writing - that is, they crossed out any words they felt they did not want, paying particular heed to unnecessary conjunctions.

- The next part of the process was to go through the writing again and put a squiggly line under any word they could perhaps change for a more interesting one, with the help of a thesaurus, also noting any places where they were unsure of the spelling.

- Second draft: Using dictionaries, thesaurus, and so on, they then wrote out their work as a poem, leaving out the crossed-out words.

- At this second draft stage they needed to find a partner. Together they conferenced, talking about the things they liked in their poems. When they had said something positive, each could then make some suggestions for change and say how they felt their partner could improve their work. After this the author of the work would make any further changes she/he felt were necesssary.

When both partners had done this, they would set about 'lining' the poems. To do this they would read their poems aloud and, every time they paused, their partner would tap on the table. Every time the reader heard a tap they would put a line-break mark (//) where the pause had occurred.

Final draft: Now the children had a piece of work to copy out in neat writing, starting a new line after every line-break mark. They made final adjustments and when the poem was completed they illustrated their work.

The children were keen to use the thesaurus, although some more work was needed on this, as they sometimes chose words that did not fit the context. The lining activity helped many children identify where they could start a new line and they often put in the line-break mark before their partner had tapped on the table. Eventually, conferencing will probably be an ideas-sharing activity or a feedback session only, and the children will be able to line and redraft independently. However, I am keen to foster this cooperative approach, as the children now see the benefit of discussion, redrafting etc.

The following examples came from this lesson:

Walking

Walking,
Walking through the river,
Splashing,
Jumping.
Feet in the water,
Picking up the sand,
Turning the water yellow.
Crackling leaves,
Swishing water,
Freezing feet,
Mud like small,
Branches flicking,
People shouting.
Walking,
Walking through the mud,
Muddy field,
Cow pat country,
Pongy smell,
Hands on nose,
Looking back where we were
before.
Walking,
Walking back to the craft.

by Matthew

Erin wrote the following poem and then went on to read examples of other poets' work. After this she looked more carefully at how to line her poems.

Feelings in the Field

Over the stile into the muddy
field
nervous and scared.
In the same field as a bull,
peering over my shoulder to see
whether it was still in its place.
It was always in the right place.
Thumping of feet on the muddy
ground.
Fear in my feet starting to crawl
up to
my head. I turned. In shock. I
saw the
Fierce bull charging. Eyes big
black balls.
Horns were big spears charging.
A giant
hairy monster charging with its
spears.
I was petrified of the monster.
Squelch,
Squelch, thump, thump.
Children running in
Fright. It stopped. Everything
was still
and calm. All I could hear was
the
mooing of the cows in the next
Field. The bull was frozen. It
glared at
us. I was shivering in my wellies.
Slowly, slowly walking away. The
bull was
gone.
Squelch, squelch away we go.

by Erin

More school journey poems

Bull

I felt scared
It was frightening
The bull was coming nearer
Getting bigger . . . bigger . . .
nearer
Hairy with fierce eyes
My heart, beating fast
My body, frozen still
I didn't move
Children ran
STOP
The children stopped
The bull stopped
Staring at us
Slowly walking off
I felt better
Was it going to chase after us
again?

by Neil

This was Neil's first attempt at poetry that he really felt satisfied with. He is a cautious child who finds it hard to concentrate, and he was very pleased with this effort.

The River

Racing with Fawwad in the deep
river
I was icy cold and soaking wet
It stung my cosy feet
I looked up and Matthew
and I heard laughing
I almost slipped, I grabbed a
grassy rock,
It was wet and slimy
Sometimes, I tasted water in
my mouth
Dirty foot prints in the mud.

by Jamie

Jamie is a reluctant writer, but he found this poem easier to do as it was connected to direct experience. He was also pleased to redraft the poem until he was completely satisfied with it.

January

During a whole school initiative on bullying we spent a lot of time talking about this issue - what we meant by bullying, what it felt like, how to deal with bullies, and so on. The children were told that they would be asked to write poems about this subject and that they should give some thought to it over a day or so. A few days later, with very little new discussion having taken place, I read these poems to the class:

Conversation Piece by Gareth Owen (Scholastic School Poems)
The Fight by Fred Sedgwick (Scholastic School Poems)
Our Side of the Playground by Eric Finney
Don't Hit Your Sister by Lesley Miranda (Poetry Jump Up)
Davy Duft by Colin McNaughton

We looked at the different forms these poets had used and the class paid attention to the way the poet's idea had led to a particular form. e.g. the conversation between the boy and his teacher. This was a popular theme and many children followed it up, but the poems that resulted were rather rambling pieces - more like stories. Rhythm featured strongly in these poems, particularly when the poem concerned children in a gang. Many of the class took on this idea and they also wanted these poems to rhyme - something they had previously moved away from. There was very little redrafting of the poems that followed. Most of the work was written in one go.

I got the Blame

Me and my sister had a fight
because she's a girl and she's
weak
   I got the blame

Me and my sister had a fight
because she lost and she cried
   I got the blame

Me and my sister had a fight
because she's younger and
fusses more than me
   I got the blame.

by Gregory

Gregory was very keen to start writing immediately after our read-aloud session. He was the first to finish and made no changes to his poem; it was exactly how he wanted it. He has received language support recently (in Year 5) and finds much of the language work difficult, but he really enjoyed this activity and took inspiration from *Don't hit your sister* by Lesley Miranda.

Girls' Gang

Miss Bossy, Jane Lang
She's the leader of the gang
Miss Skinny Ferrand
Who's second in command
Big Fat Kate
She thinks she's really great,
But can't even fit through the
school gate!
Little Miss May says she's killed
her Auntie Fay!

This is all the girls' gang
The toughest in the school
They think they're above the
rest
But they'll never pass the test!!
So . . . . if you've ever come
across . . .
Lang, Ferrand, Kate or May
Stand up to them and you'll be
   O.K!

by Naureen

Naureen made several changes to her poem before she was happy with it. She was keen for it to have marked rhyme and rhythm. It was very popular with the other children and became a class rap for a few days.

Bullying poems

Michael Pool

I know a bully his name is
Michael Pool,
He thinks he's really tough and
he thinks he's really cool.
Now this big bully, you know,
Michael Pool,
He's big and fat and hairy and
he goes to our school.
He bullies all the little kids, he
calls them horrid names,
And then he forces them to let
him join in their games.

After school it's not much
different, he's at it as soon as
he's out,
He bullies everyone he sees,
everyone who is about,
I know a bully, his name is
Michael Pool,
He thinks he's really tough and
he thinks he's really cool,
But I'll let you into my secret
Although he thinks he's tough .
. . he's really
  a fool.

by Harriet

Harriet is a talented writer and has
been a victim of quite severe bullying
in the past, so was keen to have a go
at this activity. Her work is very much
respected by the other children.

They think it's cool

They bully me each day
They laugh at me when I'm
running
They don't know they hurt me
They think it's fun
They pull my hair
They call me names.

by Deepti

Deepti is often in the role of outsider
in this difficult class. She rarely
contributes to classroom work,
preferring to watch and listen. Her
written work is not usually well
structured and her handwriting and
spelling skills are weak points. She
showed me her first draft of this
poem, which was a four line piece of
writing. We talked about ways to
redraft it, using rhythm, which she
was keen to put into her poem. We
did this on the computer, so that she
could chop the poem around without
re-writing it. This is her first piece of
writing of any length this year and she
was very pleased when it went up on
the wall. She only made a few changes
in content from her original piece. The
other children were very encouraging
about it.

This collection of poems was read to
the parallel Y6 class who were about
to write their own bullying poems.

The class teacher read from the collection I had read to my class and interspersed my class's efforts with the published poems. The children listening thought all the poems were being read aloud from books! When two readings were complete, the class teacher asked the children to respond. They all were very enthusiastic about the children's poems and in particular about Naureen's poem *Girls' Gang*.

Following on from a successful Book Week last year I decided to move the emphasis to poetry and hold a Poetry Week this year. The prospect of this filled the staff with trepidation as they felt uneasy about the whole area of teaching poetry and were unsure of what to do with the children. We began preparing for the Poetry Week during January and several ideas started to emerge.

The whole story of Poetry Week is told in a separate chapter of this book; here I only have room to print one or two of the poems that my class wrote as a consequence of the week's activity, and that are not included in that chapter.

Year 6 were particularly keen to try writing rap poetry after watching a performance by Brian Moses, using musical instruments. They began by brainstorming amongst themselves and coming up with a list of subjects to write about. These included a story involving a group of boys and a 'hip-hop cat'. The boys who wrote this took a while to get going because they were very clear about the rhythm they wanted to work to. This restricted them slightly; they had to get the

words to fit into the rhythm. The use of instruments rather took over from the actual poem, but they performed it well:

The Street Rap

This is a rap and it's all about me
I'm the Hip Hop cat and I live in a tree
A long time ago I was just about three
There was a couple of kids who were troubling me
One day I was walking down the street
I saw the same bad kids who thought they were neat
They came up to me and they pulled my tail
I OPENED MY MOUTH AND GAVE OUT A WAIL!
I'm the Hip Hop, the Hip Hop cat
I'm the Hip Hop, the Hip Hop cat
I'm the Hip Hop, the Hip Hop cat
I'm the Hip Hop Hip Hop cat.

by David, Emanuel and Sebastian

More of the raps the class wrote can be found in the chapter on 'Organising a Poetry Week'.

During Poetry Week, the class were introduced to *The Midnight Party* by Richard Edwards - a collection of poems for more than one voice. I tried to choose a variety of themes and poems for a varied number of voices. I selected a group of poems for groups

of children (mixed ability) and photocopied one for each member of the group. These were given to the groups who were then asked
1. to discuss reading as a group member and to decide on appropriate use of voice for each part.
2. to work on some particular tasks around the poem, with a view to building up a folder on that poem. Also in the folder would be the group's own edited contributions.

Poetry Week was a great success, achieving all that I hoped and much more. The children were writing poems almost from the first day of the week and were keen to try out a variety of formats. Constraints were loosened from staff and children and the result was lively discussion and performances from all around the school. A 'show and tell' session was held by staff to share good ideas and poems written by children.

March

Following on from Poetry Week, the staff were now keen to swap ideas and try teaching more poetry. A colleague of mine had done some work on 'fear' with the other Year 6 class and so I used her ideas with my class. We began by talking about what it is that makes us afraid. We all had fears to talk about, the most common of which was being alone in bed at night in the dark. Darkness seemed to be a common thread. I read the poem *The Song of the Soldier* to the class:

Here am I a soldier strong
In a war not of my making
Here am I though I hate so much
The role in death I'm taking

Here am I trapped down so deep
Under the earth that's quaking
Here am I alone, afraid
Seeing my own hands shaking

Here am I, so full of fear
My tired limbs are aching
Here am I - death is so near
It's through my body shaking

My pain is great
My terror real
But when death comes
I shall not feel
  - but peace.

The children were very touched by this powerful piece and much mature discussion followed. We talked about:

who was the soldier?

where was the place underground?

why was he 'trapped'?

what kind of death did he fear?

when was the war that this poem relates to?

We looked at the structure of the poem and the children identified other poems that used a similar structure very quickly. Then we built up a word bank on the board of 'fear' words.

From a large collection of words, children were asked to select ten of their choice that they would use in a poem. We also talked about the colour of fear - they could choose one colour and add it to their list of fear words. Many children were conversant with imagery but most were not, so we talked about metaphors and how they could make writing more alive. Now, using these words, the children were asked to build some lines around their chosen theme - using the same cues as before: what? who? why? where? when? The structure was left to the children - all managed to write a poem.

Some individuals

Martin
Martin was not very animated during the discussion but wanted to talk to me about being afraid of the dark in bed at night. We talked about the things he did to reassure himself or to ease his fear. They were: keeping the light on, hiding under the covers with his teddy, and keeping the TV on so that there was a noise. Martin said he heard noises he didn't like, and the TV would drown the noises too.
1st draft:

Scared of the Dark

At night when I go to bed I
keep my light on
because I am scared of the dark

At night when I go to bed I hide
under the covers
because I am scared of the dark.

At night when I go to bed I turn
on the t.v. because I do not
want to hear noises because I
am scared of the dark.

In this first draft, Martin was keen to create a pattern or rhythm. There were three things he was afraid of, so he decided to create three verses to his poem. The final draft was decorated and mounted in a class book

Sebastian

Sebastian is always full of enthusiasm and interest for his work but is quite often disappointed by the end result. He was full of ideas for his poem - he wanted it to be about being trapped in a dark alley.

Using his word bank, his first attempt went as follows:

> I'm scared of the dark
>
> because dogs go bark bark,
>
> I'm scared of the dark
>
> because there's a thing in the park
>
> I'm scared of the night
>
> because I always have a fright
>
> I'm scared of the night
>
> Because I see no light.

When we read this aloud together, Sebastian was disappointed with the result and didn't know how to improve it. We talked again about the who? what? where? questions and he made a second draft:

> Here I am in the year 2000
>
> In an alleyway and it's dark
>
> Here I am on the street
>
> With lots of fear
>
> Here I am, feeling afraid and
>
> people coming to me.

We talked again about using imagery, something Sebastian had been working on that week. He also thought that posing the questions in the poem would be interesting and using the senses to tell what was happening.

He was justly proud of his final draft.

Walking ~~down~~ an alley

Walking down an alley late at night.

I hear a big noise it gave me a fright

could it be a gangster coming my way?

My heart starts to pound

and my feet starts to run

I'd better slow down because

my feet are like a drum

what about the gangster has

he got a gun?

I wish it was daylight with

a bright orange sun

This dark alleyway makes me

want to run.

by Sebastian

35

Jamie

Jamie worked up to this final draft. First he made a list and then he wrote a first draft. He liked the idea of an echo and changed the beginning of his draft so that he could use the echo idea.

Naureen

Naureen is a keen reader with a good grasp of ideas and has written some beautiful poetry this year. Her poem on a 'Home Alone' theme was strongly imagined.

Radhika

Radhika had only one attempt at this atmospheric poem:

I am a homeless girl, alone
I am on the dark side of the
streets, no home
afraid of the dangers that lurk
through the streets
could there be somebody
following me?

twitering night birds and
footsteps I hear,

are the footsteps far?
or entering near?

No hot dinner to eat
So cold I can't sleep

the cold harsh wind,
rushing through my hair

no parents to love me,
nobody to care!

July

SATs, reports, and a school drama production unfortunately pushed poetry to the bottom of the list of activities this term. However, just before we broke up we wrote some poems on taking risks. This was inspired by an incident involving my twelve year old daughter. She is not allowed out of school at lunchtime, but was seen by a prefect in the chip shop! The prefect told her dad, who is a friend of the family, and word got back to us. When my daughter was tackled, she was mightily indignant that she had been rumbled, but spoke about the excitement of taking a risk like that.

I told this story to my class who were very interested in someone else getting into trouble! Taking risks was something they had all done. We spoke about all sorts of circumstances, such as stealing sweets/cakes from the kitchen cupboards, leaving the TV on in their bedrooms when they had been told not to, escaping when they had been 'grounded', jumping into a river they had been told not to play near, running across a road or even crossing a road they had been told not to cross. Each child had a story to tell and we had a long and animated discussion about the sorts of risks we all take. We spoke about how it feels and what we think about when we take risks. I explained that what was in my daughter's head was not necessarily what came out of her mouth!

The resulting poems touched on a range of experiences the children had had. They could all identify with taking risks.

Postscript

The year ended here, but I was particularly pleased, during the following school year, to be given copies of these poems by children from my class who were now in Year 7 at a new school. They are poems that pick up on the bullying theme that we had worked on, but show obvious signs of increased maturity and control. I was told by the secondary English teacher at the new school that this quality of writing was achievable only because of all the work we had done during our poetry year. We rarely see what happens when the children we teach move on, so this was a particularly gratifying postscript to the year.

The Bully

I stepped into the playground
I hoped she wasn't there
the one who laughed when I fell
the one who didn't care.

I stepped into the playground
I hoped she wasn't there
the one who took my sweets away
and pushed me off my chair.

I stepped into the playground
I hoped she wasn't there
I'd like to hit her back someday
But I know I wouldn't dare.

by Vicky

But they were waiting

I went to school late
but they were waiting.
I hid my money,
but they found it.
I did my work really well,
but they ripped it up.
I got them in trouble,
but they got me back.
I fell over and got badly hurt,
but they just laughed.
I ran to my gate,
but they were standing outside.
I came into my house,
and they weren't there.

by Matthew

Varina Emblen
Penwortham Primary School
London Borough of Wandsworth

Not quite Tennyson

Julia Gatt

Autumn, and a new school year stretching ahead. After four years of teaching in Key Stage 1, I had changed to a mixed Year 4/5 class and I was hoping I could rise to the challenge. Although I had taught this age range at my previous school some years before, the curriculum had changed a lot since then. The intake at my present school included many able and well-motivated children and I knew that providing work for them was going to demand a great deal of research and planning.

The first few weeks started well. Autumn brought 'Harvest' celebrations and the obligatory school celebrations followed. 'Poetry!' I thought. It seemed an opportunity for each child to do their bit, rather than allowing the spotlight to fall on a selected few. Our topic was 'Food', so this became the subject of the children's poems. They decided independently on the organisation of their own poetry-writing - some chose to write an individual piece, others wrote in groups. When the poems were completed, the writers decided how they were going to be performed. Apart from deciding the performing order, they organized themselves totally. I was really pleased with the results which were diverse in style and in performance:

Lumpy mash potato

I hate mash
Especially when it's lumpy!
My sister loves it.
She opens her mouth.
And shows me.
It makes me
SICK!

Do You Like Chocolate?

Do you like chocolate
or do you like peas?
do you feel like stuffing your face
with yummy scrummy cheese?
Well chocolate's real lovely
and peas are a treat
and cheese makes me happy
(I also like meat)
The worst food for me
would have to be
honey and treacle
They're really sickly!
Ah, yes, I like peas,
and yummy scrummy cheese
and beans can be quite pleasant,
but really there's only one food
made for me
and that's
C-H-O-C-O-L-A-T-E
CHOCOLATE!
Ah, yes, I'm sure,
that that must be
the only food made for me -
tell you what though
if I eat much more
I'll need to go on a diet
wouldn't that be a bore!

There were several favourable remarks from staff. 'And that's before you've even started your poetry course!' observed the Deputy Head. 'It's obvious you've read a wide variety of poetry to them already.' I hadn't, but I received the congratulations with a self-satisfied glow.

It served me right for being so cocky! I deluded myself into thinking that if the class could achieve all that by themselves, they would be able to produce even more exciting results under my expert guidance. But after such a good start, what came immediately after this was downhill for quite some time.

I began the poetry course, but things didn't turn out as I expected. Although we went on writing poetry in the class, somehow, with me controlling the whole process, the results were flat and uninspired. I didn't know what had gone wrong.

For example, one week, after listening to one teacher discussing her class's response to Grace Nichols' poem about the sun, I decided I would like to use it as a starting point for some poetry with my children. I read the poem to them, we had some discussion about possible comparisons and the use of imagery. But what they went on to write was the very opposite of the diverse range of poetry that they had achieved in the beginning. Some of them were certainly well written, as these examples show:

Amy is like the calm sea,
quietly bumping into the rocks
Washing away shells and crabs
and gets angry when the sun
goes in
Working and working silently on
the
life of herself.

Sam is like a mountain
with a waterfall
plunging down
all calm
not worrying
unless he's being chased by
girls.
He's like a lizard
scurrying along
always in a rush
always running around
and chatting
but still a great friend.

The poems contained the essential elements we had discussed, and showed that the children had understood what was expected of them. But they were all too much the same. The spark of individuality had gone. I had shown them how a poem should be written and they had obliged. Somehow, I got the feeling this wasn't honest writing; rather than being felt it seemed to be manufactured.

I also noticed as the term wore on that it was the small group of boys in the class who were most disaffected. The class was very female-dominated; it contained twenty-three girls and only eleven boys. Both physically and academically the boys were isolated. It was noticeable that they always sat in a large group together, like survivors on a life raft. I needed to find a way to motivate and unite the class.

I discussed this the next time the poetry workshop group met, and the idea of performance poetry was raised. Like most children, mine were natural performers. The group suggested that I remove the onus of writing for a time and just concentrate on the reading and performing of poetry.

Most of the girls were positive about this right from the start - in fact they loved it. They chose their poems with care, clamoured to perform in the weekly 'sharing' assembly, planned their outfits and props with meticulous care, and practised at every opportunity. Initially, enthusiasm among the boys was much less evident. Although they enjoyed the process of selecting material, they seemed to get hung up on sound effects. Every piece had to be accompanied by loud percussion instruments. More dialogue and dissent occurred over who was going to play the favourite instruments than over any aspect of the actual poetry reading. I tried very hard to just let it ride. This time I was determined to let the process evolve in a more gradual way.

Boys and poetry

A lot of the poetry chosen by the boys was of the rap variety and, though they enjoyed the rehearsals, when it came to actually performing in front of an audience they chickened out. I was heartened, however, to find they had actually written their own rap, although they were reluctant to give public performances of it. Whilst the rap itself was not particularly great, the performance they gave in the classroom certainly was. (The sound effects were wonderful, and yet there was not a percussion instrument in sight!) But they could not be persuaded to repeat this for a larger audience.

After two sharing assemblies had passed without a performance, in spite of many rehearsals having been held during the week, Tim finally said one Thursday morning, 'I'll do it on my own'. He did, and his performance was terrific. He was confident, and paced himself well, resisting the temptation to rush through the piece, and producing the most marvellous sound effects. The response from the rest of the school was very enthusiastic, and you could see Tim relaxing and beginning to really enjoy himself.

A few weeks later, I brought in a 'moods' tape for a dance session and played a track (which was the theme from *Twin Peaks*). Since my intention was to focus on dance, the idea of writing initially didn't arise in this session. We talked about how body language expressed emotion and as time went on, each group devised a mime sequence to go with the music. Most chose to portray a scene they would find particularly sad, or which they thought related well to the music in some way. One group chose to enact a bullying scene, another the death of someone they were close to.

In one group of boys, the conversation moved to the death of a pet, particularly if it had to be put down. We talked some more about this as a class, and then each group showed the rest their initial ideas and children commented on their interpretation. They pointed out the parts they thought worked well and made suggestions for ways to improve other parts. Then it occurred to me to suggest that they should write down their feelings, from the viewpoint of the role they were playing. The results of this came out as poetry. Several of the poems were very strong and we realised that they, too, were well worthy of sharing with the school.

The children planned how this poetry could be incorporated into their mimes. A couple of groups decided the music should be turned down so that it was playing quietly in the background. Then the mime scene would freeze while the poem was read. Another group, portraying the bullying incident, arranged that each group member should read a piece of poetry reflecting the feelings of the individual characters in the incident at the end of the performance.

But it was Tim, writing as the owner of a dog about to be put down, that literally brought tears to the eyes of some staff:

When I saw the look on the vet's face
I felt doubtful
then he said
it was just like I imagined it.
I felt awful
but I let him go.
I heard him yelp as he went
he doesn't have a clue
he's been a good dog while it lasted
when I looked at him
I saw him as a puppy
as though I had just bought him
I saw sadness in his big brown eyes
I ran my fingers through his soft fur for the last time
and sadly walked out.

I would like to say that from then on, we have gone from strength to strength but that would not be totally honest. As in so many aspects of school life, some children have developed so that they now see poetry as a natural way of expressing ideas in all sorts of areas, whilst others still have to be directed and persuaded, not necessarily during the actual writing of it, but in order to see it as a first choice when an experience needs to be described.

Art week

The greatest satisfaction I experienced, though, occurred during 'Art Week' which took place in one of the last weeks of the school year. The week was well under way, and a variety of artists from every sphere had descended upon the school. Helen Wilkes had agreed to be our 'Artist in Residence' for the week and brought with her paintings from her current exhibition entitled 'Childhood Fragments'. They portrayed glimpses of childhood memories familiar to most of us. There was one of her having her cheek pinched playfully by a relative, another of walking along the road with her mother, holding her favourite panda and grasping only her mother's finger. These pictures lent themselves naturally to poetry, and the children produced a good selection of work in response both to individual paintings and to their overall theme.

But what stuck in my mind was what Helen Wilkes said about the features that make an artist. She pointed out that most of us consider people who could draw and paint well as being 'good at art', but she explained that was only a small part of artistic skill. What really made an artist, she thought, were the feelings and emotions they put into their work, and the fact that they chose to express themselves in this medium. How you respond to pictures, she explained, is a vital part of this process of developing a visual sensibility. Becoming aware of what you notice when you look at a picture is part of becoming an artist.

I remembered an occasion in the previous year when the Art adviser for Bexley, Dan China, had chaired a meeting at our school. When we went into the staffroom, we were instructed to sit around a painting he had propped up on a cupboard. In turn, we had to get up, go over to the painting and say 'I can see . . . . '. Initially that proved no problem; there was a fair amount of detail in the picture. However, we were expected to continue long after all of the obvious things had been mentioned and we began to search feverishly around the painting for some small detail someone else had overlooked. Finally, we were pointing out the tiniest symbols, shafts of light or perceived shadows. This, of course, was the object of the exercise. We were being led into a way of looking which was not merely a question of glancing and attempting to absorb the whole picture in one go, but involved a careful study and awareness of the detail, light and shadow that go to make up the whole.

So I decided to do the same thing with my class. Rebecca Penny, who organised our 'Art Week', has a beautiful painting at home, painted by her father, which she offered to lend to us. It was perfect because it is a triptych which opens up to reveal three paintings of an area of Shrewsbury at different times of the day. It had plenty of detail and lots of specific things to comment on before moving on to the more abstract elements.

The children started off in the way we had during our staff meeting. Again, once all the main details had been exhausted, they eagerly scanned the painting for something that had been missed. And then they began to add dimensions of their own to this exercise, suggesting perhaps thoughts that a person might be thinking, or motives for a particular action. At the end of the hour we spent talking about the painting, I suggested they wrote something about it.

I suddenly noticed Grant. Everyone has got or has had a Grant in their class. He has difficulties with basic skills, usually lacks motivation, spends two hours looking for a pencil, is rarely on task for more than minutes at a time. But there he suddenly was, pencil in hand, and he was writing! And this is what he produced:

> I can see a buoy bobbing in the lake
> A shrimp in the company of fish
> The North Star sparkling at night
> I can see a man and a woman kissing
> I can see a beer belly on a bench.

Not quite Tennyson, but wonderful nevertheless.

Julia Gatt
Dulverton Primary School
London Borough of Bexley

Joining the Poetry Club

I was interested in taking part in this workshop project because of my rather ambivalent attitude towards poetry. I knew that, like eating your greens, it was good for you, yet despite having studied it at college I still didn't feel comfortable with it. A bit like the inexperienced readers that Frank Smith described as not yet belonging to the literacy club, I felt somehow puzzled and inadequate in relation to it. As a consequence I didn't feel enthusiastic or confident enough to use poetry in my teaching.

As a member of a pupil support service, I support inexperienced readers and writers throughout key stages one and two, working either with whole classes in partnership with the class teacher, or with small groups. During the poetry workshop year I worked mainly with year five classes and year two groups, although the approach I developed could be used throughout the key stages.

I began in a year five class where two children were at stage 3 of the Code of Practice, mainly because of inappropriate behaviour. One child was behaviourally very unpredictable and found it difficult to collaborate in any group activity, sometimes even in class activities. The other, a bilingual child, was very withdrawn, rarely speaking or making any contributions in class discussions. There was also a group of eight children who were at stages 1 and 2 of the Code of Practice because of concern about their literacy achievement. I hoped to cater for these divergent needs through the medium of poetry. My aim was to create learning situations which would

Jenny Vernon

support discussion and collaborative achievement at the same time as encouraging and celebrating the individual voice of each child.

I began by dipping my toe in gradually, beginning with poems based on simple statements and continuing with the part of poetry where I already felt enthusiastic and confident, namely rhymes and songs with a pronounced rhythmical pattern, sometimes supported by actions. As the project proceeded I became more adventurous, using ideas generated by the poetry group's regular meetings and by a selection of published poems, as a stimulus for the children to compose their own poetry.

The first class topic of the year was Carnival and as this particular school is situated in North Kensington, part of the Notting Hill Carnival route, most of the children had first hand experience of it. They had also recently taken part in a carnival workshop led by Alex Pascal, a well known Caribbean storyteller and carnival enthusiast.

We began by discussing the images that carnival evoked for each child, and how they were experienced via the senses. Then, working in groups of four, each child contributed one line beginning 'Carnival is . . .' to a group poem. They conferenced each other, suggesting alternative lines where necessary, and finally deciding on a sequence for the four lines. The class then came together to read out the verses and decide on the sequence for the whole-class poem.

Carnival is . . . .

- mad, sugar cane, reggae
- the pavement is moving
- my heart is going thump thump
- pay the devil, jab jab

Carnival is . . .
- brilliant to see
- nice for me
- out in the streets
- where everybody meets

Carnival is . . .
- jungle music
- where everyone dances
- people wearing masks
- small children get lost and policemen find them

The finished poem was displayed around the classroom so that every child could feel a sense of achievement as they read, re-read and discussed their own and others' contributions.

Moving away from rhyme

Taking an idea which Michael Rosen had introduced to the poetry workshop group I moved away from the set structures and asked the children to think of a place that they were familiar with and imagine themselves there, thinking about what they could see, hear, feel, taste, and registering any inner thoughts they might have. These different sense experiences were then mapped out onto the profile of a face which they drew on a piece of A3 paper. The children's reaction was at first to record details like 'people talking' or 'smell of food', without being specific or noting actual speech or particular food smells in a way which would make their writing more immediate and interesting.

I found this technique especially useful for very inexperienced or reluctant writers, as they could draw their responses as well as using words. This enabled them to include details which would have been lost if they had had to translate their thoughts into writing. The outline of the face on the page provided a physical container for the elements of the poem, and gave the writer an overview of the experience. This helped them on to the next stage of the process which was to decide how to sequence the information in the 'map' and turn it into a poem.

I used this picture map format successfully with a group of inexperienced, year two writers. They were able to think of places very easily and I noticed, as with older children,

the breadth of detail they included, which they might not have done if they had had to laboriously write it all down. At first, some children chose not to write at all, but only to draw. This time I modelled the drafting process by actually scribing for them, writing the results of the shared writing up on the computer, and taking it back to them to see if they wanted to make any changes. Finally I presented them with printed versions, which they illustrated and practised reading for a performance to the rest of the class.

When we came along to doing the second 'place poem' all of the children had the confidence to complete the whole of the transcription for themselves, beginning with the brainstorm, and then drafting and redrafting the finished poems. I was interested to see the influence of what they had read coming into their own compositions. This illustrated the point that learners need worthwhile texts on which to model their own writing.

Poems not yet on the Underground

Because of the influence of the poetry workshop I was becoming more aware of poetry on the radio and poetry in general. Opening a copy of *Poems on the Underground* that I found on a friend's bookshelf, and flicking through the pages to find the ones that I had often pondered and savoured between stops, gave me the idea of a specific context and 'audience' for the poems the children were beginning to write. I planned a project called 'Poems not yet on the Underground'. I was attracted to this broadsheet way of displaying poems for a general audience.

In class we discussed the different purposes and varieties of reading to be found on the Underground and why advertisers like to use the inside of tube trains. I introduced the children to the fact that poems were also displayed in the trains. Not all of the children had noticed them. I explained that they could consider their own poems as being future reading material to brighten up the lives of weary tube travellers.

Together we read a selection of poem posters which I had bought from the London Transport museum. As well as being good examples of published poetry, the poems illustrated points of knowledge about language. Here is the selection:

1. *The Cries of London* Anon
This series of street traders' calls illustrates the practical use of rhymes as a way of handing on an oral tradition in the days when not very many people were literate.

2. *The Silver Swan* Anon
This poster makes the link between lyrics and poetry by setting out the 15th century madrigal text, accompanied by the music, next to the modern version.

3. *Anthem for Doomed Youth* Wilfred Owen
As well as being a very powerful poem, this poster includes the poet's handwritten draft alongside the final version, making the point that drafting is part of the writing process.

4. *The Twa Corbies* Anon
This Scottish ballad is a wonderfully gory story of two crows planning to pick a fallen knight's bones clean, and also shows how different Englishes have evolved over the centuries.

5. *A Song for England* Andrew Salkey
This impression of England from a Caribbean perspective is another example of the existence today of other Englishes.

6. *A Picture* Bei Dao
This Chinese poem is shown both in the original and in the translated text, and illustrates how different languages can have different scripts.

Working in mixed ability groups of five, with the more experienced supporting the less experienced, the children were asked to read through one poem and, with one person acting as scribe, to record the title and author and their responses under the following headings:

- What did you think about the poem when you read it for the first time?
- Did you notice anything special about it?
- Which part did you like the best?
- Was there anything that puzzled you?
- What did you think when you read it again?

This is a modification of Aidan Chambers' approach described in *Tell Me*, *Children Reading and Talk*. As a way of getting started, it works very well. This activity generated a lot of discussion and negotiation of shared and individual meanings for each poem.

I was relieved and pleasantly surprised at the children's reactions. Unlike myself (who had always approached poetry with the undermining fear of not being able to understand it) they confidently and assertively set about making meaning from it. The first readings were generally rather negative with comments like:

'It was too long and had a funny title' (*Twa Corbies*)
'Quite boring' (*The Cries of London Town*)
'I thought it was French till the end'
'It doesn't make sense' (*Song for England*)
'I didn't understand a word of it'
'I do not understand words but some words good' (*A Picture*)

but through subsequent readings, which were necessary to answer the next questions, they began to modify their opinions. Nearly all of them, in response to the last question, showed that they had started to make something of it:
'Some bits quite funny' (*Cries of London*)
'When I heard it the second time I understood more than what I understood first' (*The Picture*)
'I understood it' (*Twa Corbies*)
'I really got to enjoy it once we read it the second time' (*A Song for England*)

Apart from encouraging thinking about poetry, this work enabled the children to make explicit a lot of their knowledge about language. One child began to give a simultaneous translation of *Two Corbies* as she read it out, another remarked of *A Song for England* 'It sounds like someone who has just begun to learn English.'

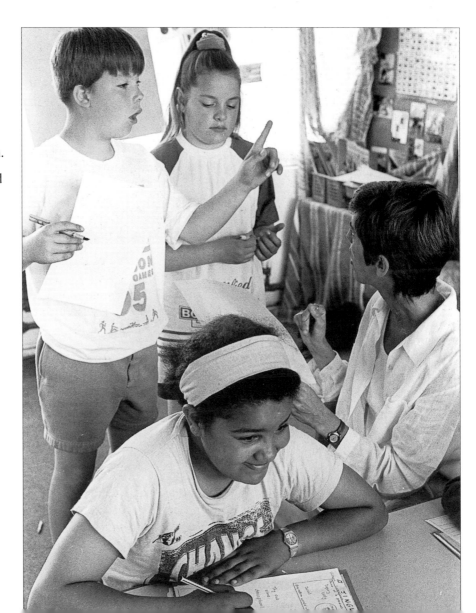

Imaginary others

When travelling home on the tube (how else?) from the first meeting of the poetry workshop I opened the copy of Jackie Kay's book of children's poetry, *Two's Company* which we had been given to read. I was delighted and surprised that I could relate to all of it and actually recognised one of the poems I had heard and enjoyed on the radio. My most exciting discovery was that Jackie Kay hadn't begun each new line with a capital letter!

Two poems I found particularly evocative were: *The Adventures of Carla Johnson* and *Two Carla Johnsons*. I was immediately reminded of a painting I had recently seen, *The Two Fridas* by the Mexican artist Frida Kahlo, which portrays two striking images of herself. An excerpt from her diary next to it explains how, since early childhood, she had an imaginary companion who, unlike the real Frida, was happy and healthy.

I read these two poems aloud at school to see if I could tap into the world of the children's imaginary selves as a stimulus for writing poetry. I began by reading *The Adventures of Carla Johnson*, asking the children to listen out for any parts they particularly liked or anything they wanted to comment on. They were puzzled why it had taken half an hour for her to get back into bed after closing the door, but liked the image of 'the cat's miaow of the door'. Although the inevitable conclusion from some was that it was 'only a dream' the majority felt that maybe a magical friend had come to visit.

Before reading *Two Carla Johnsons* I asked them to listen for details of both girls. After reading it through once, I asked for descriptions of the two and began to assemble a rough sketch on the board incorporating all the details as the children gave them. The sketch showed two stick figures, one with hands and a tower block in the background, facing the other who had wings framed by a rainbow. Reading the poem a second time elicited more details which were all added to the composite picture.

Having presented the content of the poem graphically for the benefit of the bilingual children in the class, I again invited comments and enquired whether there really were two Carla Johnsons. The children decided that maybe one was 'in the other one's head', 'an imaginary friend'. Then followed a series of contributions about imagined friends and siblings. It was amazing how many children could offer examples, involving themselves or others in their families, of imaginary companions. Extra places were set at the table, parents were asked to move up on the bus to leave space, conversations were overheard on a swing, all involving these imaginary others.

I asked the class to think about the imaginary friend they had already had or to imagine one they might have. I gave them a worksheet with prompts such as 'looks like', 'likes', 'can', 'special because' as a framework for their brainstorm about the characteristics of this imaginary friend.

I have found these two poems extremely enabling as a way of unlocking children's imaginations and have used them on many subsequent occasions, every time being really impressed by what was produced.

The two Azizas

Aziza watches Power Rangers
every day on the tele.
At night the other Aziza goes
flying through the sky.

Aziza likes swimming but she's
not very good.

At night Aziza goes swimming in
the ocean with the big fish.

Aziza never goes on holiday but
the other Aziza goes to Somalia

every weekend.

My Special Friend

My special friend is my dad
because I haven't seen him in a
long time.

Sometimes
I dream we're doing all the fun
things together.

Sometimes
it's like a dream come true.

But when I wake up in the
morning it makes me so upset

Sometimes I cry and
sometimes it feels so natural.

Only one of me

Another poem which I found useful as
a starting point was James Berry's *One*.
After reading the poem to the class
and discussing wonderful lines like:

'Only one of me
and nobody can get a second
one
from a photocopy machine'

the children brainstormed about
themselves. This included completing
the phrases:
'no one has . . . . like me
no one can . . . . .like me'
This gave the less confident members
of the class the opportunity to reflect
on themselves as individuals.

There's only one of me

No one has eyes like me
with lovely long eye lashes.

No one reads like me
fast and furious.

No one eats like me
in two seconds flat.

No one can make a carnival float
like me
with fantastic ideas.

Sometimes I used the children's
relationships with other people as a
starting point. I usually devised a
simple worksheet which served to
stimulate and organise their thoughts
before they moved on to the first draft
of their poem.

Reading and responding

I found myself scouring through anthologies looking for poems which I thought would interest the children. I was opened up to a world of poetry which I hadn't really been interested in or made time for previously and found myself on a bit of a 'voyage of discovery'. I photocopied the poems, mounted them on a coloured card and eventually had a collection which also included children's own poems, large enough for a whole class to choose from. After browsing through them, working in pairs, they were asked to respond to those they had selected again in a similar way to that suggested by Aidan Chambers, under the following headings:

- Title/author
- What's the poem about?
- What does the poet want to say?
- What would you like to say to the poet?
- Does it rhyme?
- Draw something the poem makes you think of.

I found this a valuable way of encouraging them to look more closely at poems. They each chose a particular favourite and, after practising, presented it to the class. Each child selected one of their own poems which was printed out in a landscape format like the ones on the underground. These were made into a class anthology and we sent examples to the London Transport museum with a suggestion that they might like to choose some for their future tube displays.

The child with the acting-out behaviour had not been miraculously transformed by the poetry sessions but she did manage to co-operate in a group and contribute to class discussions and find enjoyment in poetry. The withdrawn child gained in confidence and was eventually prepared to read out her work in front of the class. The class itself views poetry as something enjoyable and relevant to them, and they see themselves as poets.

I am no longer hesitant to use poetry in my teaching and now consider it to be a very valuable medium which is especially enabling for bilingual children who have a greater repertoire of sounds and rhythms to draw on, and for less confident or less experienced readers and writers who are able to succeed because of the concise, personal nature of poetry.

Personal voices

I found that beginning with quite mundane yet rhythmical verses, encouraging the children to make up their own jingles and hear their own speech rhythms, gave them a basis on which to try out progressively more sophisticated, personal writing. One child in particular who, prior to the poetry sessions, rarely ever finished a piece of work and was invariably to be heard in the middle of a verbal vendetta whenever the teacher wanted the class to be quiet, progressed over a period of three months from a rather pedestrian yet humorous version of *Miss Mary Mac* :

> My mummy said said said
> now go to bed bed bed
> so I said no no no
> and she turned red red red
> Mummy said now now now
> so I said no no no
> My mummy said said said
> I'll throw you in bed bed bed
> so I said no no no
> and she said oh oh oh
> Now it's morning morning
> morning
> and I am still yawning yawning
> yawning
> My mum shout shout shout
> go to school school school
> So I said NO!

to writing poems of a very personal nature:

Me

> I'm on my own
> I need someone to
> talk to. What if I die
> what if something
> happens to me.
> I'm scared. I want
> to die, but the
> world ain't over I
> want to live somehow
> and I want to die somehow.
> This is the end of the
> world should I kill
> myself or should I
> let myself die.
> I'm dying in a small
> house on my own help me
> please, some one.

She now sees herself as a poet and has experienced a sense of achievement on which she can build as a learner.

Throughout the course of the poetry project I have been able to re-assess my appreciation of poetry alongside the children I have been teaching. Above all I have learned the important lesson of being able to tolerate not understanding everything, yet still reading on. I know now that poetry is like other media and that one can exercise personal choice, rather than feeling obliged to appreciate and understand everything that is presented as part of our literary heritage. I have learned to hear the human voices behind the poems and to be more assertive in my own evaluation of poetry.

Although I doubt I'll ever be found clutching a copy of *The Waste Land* to my bosom I have discovered other voices that speak to me.

Jenny Vernon
Pupil Support Service
Royal Borough of Kensington and Chelsea

A personal journey

I am not a particularly literary type of person. I didn't read much as a child. Beyond nursery rhymes I didn't have much experience of poetry at all. It was only my college years, coinciding with the sixties and the emergence of the Liverpool poets with their popularising of poetry, that started me on a personal journey and made me want to open up to children the enjoyment of poetry as early as possible. I did not want this enjoyment to have to wait till they were as old as I was, or risk it passing them by.

I came on Michael Rosen's poetry workshop course because for the last two years I had had classes that produced lovely poetry. I expected to find new ideas and come to understand more about the process of 'teaching' - 'getting' poetry out of children. I thought that because I had had these two poetically-inclined classes, this process might be one of osmosis - my love of poetry seeping out of me and producing poets.

When I got my class at the beginning of the workshop year I decided to do some poetry on Space, to complement a science project. I found some poems to read - a collection written by Charles Cornell - but these proved a poor inspiration. When the children produced their first drafts I was horrified to realise that what they were producing was prose, not poetry. This had never happened to me before. Pages of description, with no form, pattern, feeling, rhyme or conciseness of thought. The class did not have in their minds the concept of a poem, and I had taken it for granted that all children came equipped with this knowledge and ability.

So I stopped expecting them to produce poetry and set about a concerted campaign to introduce and familiarise them with poetry.

I took every opportunity to read poetry with and to them. But it was more than just the reading of poetry, they needed to see how the poem was arranged and laid out, and to know what a poem looked like. I got as many poetry books as possible to put amongst their reading books so that they could choose them to read.

After a period of familiarisation, and giving them plenty of warning, I asked the children to choose their favourite poem. This brought in a wonderful selection of poems, thirty different poems, some funny, some sad, some long and telling a story, some short little ditties. The children read them to each other, then wrote them out in their best handwriting and illustrated them. They also had to write a piece saying why they liked this poem best. The poems were mounted and displayed in the hall and in the library area outside the classroom so that they and others could read and re-read them at their leisure.

Maria Maguire

Getting used to poetry

From other teachers in the CLPE workshop I picked up many ideas about how to familiarise children with poetry:

• To have the children's poetry displayed around the school like their art work. One teacher said she calls this 'Poems not yet on the underground'.

• To give all the children a chance to choose a 'poem of the week'. They write it up, illustrate it (if they want to) and say why they chose it, and then share it with the class. After that it can be displayed for the week.

• To find an area of wall board that can be freely used by children to display things of interest from home, and to encourage children to display poems that they have written in their own time.

• To write class poems - that is a poem written by the whole class, everyone contributing a word or a line, then discussing the order of the lines and arranging them as the class feel they sound best.

• To organise poetry writing in groups, so that the responsibility and enjoyment for the end result is shared.

• To invite the class to perform published poetry or their own poetry, using drama and sound effects.

The writing of a class poem proved to be one of the most effective ways of demonstrating how to go about writing poetry and directing attention to the look of a poem.

Poems about sounds

One of the first class poems we did was on sounds. First I read Gareth Owen's poem *Half Asleep*, then I asked the children to fold their arms, rest their heads on their arms, shut their eyes and just listen to the sounds around them. After a few minutes of this we wrote down all the sounds we had heard, with everyone making a contribution. We decided to arrange the sentences into groups:

> sounds they made
> sounds around them
> the interruption we had
> and far away sounds

starting and finishing with the instructions that I had given them. Here is the poem that was written as a result of this session:

The Sound of Silence

Arms folded.
Head down.
Eyes shut.
What can you hear?

My heart gently beating
A rumble in my tummy.
A swallow, a sigh.
The ticking of my watch.
My breath going in and out.

A cough
A giggle
A stifled yawn.

Hollie shuffling
Matthew sniffing
Adam's chair scraping
Ishmael blowing raspberries.
People finding it hard to be quiet.

A knock on the door
The door opens
Footsteps
A request for paper
A reply
The sliding of the paper tray
The rustling of the paper
Footsteps
The door closes.

Chattering, nattering out in the hall.
Screams in the playground.

Right, sit up
Eyes open
What did you hear?

by Class 6B

The poem was written up and everyone had a copy. 'That was easy' was the children's comment, but this experience seemed to get us over the hurdle of feeeling that poetry was too hard and that 'I can't do it!'

The following weekend I asked the children to go somewhere where they could be alone, sometime over the weekend, and again lie down, shut their eyes and listen to what they heard. Then they would record the sounds and lay them out as a poem.

I was really pleased with the results. All the children, from those who have difficulty writing to the very able children, produced poems they were really proud of:

I Thought it was Quiet

I thought it was quiet until I
heard
the radio going
the wind blowing.
The sound of an aeroplane
and voices talking now and
again.
The washing machine spinning
and the iron shhhing
and I'm coughing.
Footsteps thumping.
The sound of a bird
that's what I heard.

by Matthew

We wrote a few poems like this. It's a very good basis for an immediate response poem.

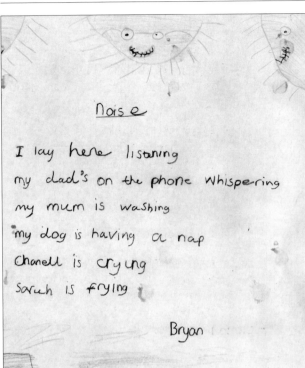

Noise

I lay here listening
my dad's on the phone whispering
my mum is washing
my dog is having a nap
Chanell is crying
Sarah is frying

Bryan

The Almost Silent Front Room

I hear myself breathing,
As the the clock ticks by,
Cars drive past.
The screeching of brakes,
Of a distant car
And on the T.V.
The advert for Corn Pops is on
you see, so
"You can't stop a corn popper
popping more corn!!"

by Alex

Sounds in the Silence

Seems like silence all around me
But then the little noises come
At first all I hear is me breathing
But then my Mum gives a sigh
And the friendly hiss of our gas fire
Plus the clock ticking on and on
Then bath water starts to run
And some scraping from down stairs
But all the time the wind is blowing
And the rain is falling fast outside.

Gregory

Shared experience

The most rewarding part of teaching poetry was that all the class could produce work they were pleased with, proud to share, and which received praise from the other children. This was especially good for the children who found written language in other forms, like stories, arduous.

One day we had a fire alert; the whole school had to be evacuated and the fire services called. When we got back to class I gave out big pieces of sugar paper. The children sat in groups and each group had to nominate one person to scribe for the group. This person was given a big felt tip pen and as a group they wrote down what they said, felt and so on, during the fire alert. Then they were given another piece of sugar paper where they ordered their ideas into a poem.

These were then displayed in the classroom. Eventually they were written up, mounted in a book with a cover of licking flames and put in the library for all to read:

Fire Alert

We all thought it was a false alarm
We were worried. What would happen to our things?
Also we thought,
What would happen?
Would we have to have time off school?
Or would we have to change schools?
Another thought was,
Is there anyone in the school?
People were hot, thirsty
And needed the loo.
Some children were in the middle of P.E.
And had to wait half dressed in the canteen.

by Chloe, Samantha, Naomi and Charlene

One really good starting point for writing is to get children to write about themselves. We read a poem called *Grown Ups* from *The Cadbury's Book of Children's Poetry*. The theme of the poem is how adults talk to children. Then we had an animated discussion on how parents, grandparents, brothers and sisters, and lodgers spoke to children.

I asked the children to record a few examples of what certain people in their family say to them. This produced lots of really lovely poems especially this one by Sara:

Grown-ups!

My Mum says
'Get out of my face
I'm trying to watch tele'
'But mum'
'No buts'.

My uncle says
'Take the dog out'
'But I've got no one to go with'
'The dog's going with you!'

My teacher says
'Not now, I'm too busy'
So I take
my problem
away.

by Sara

Sara was so boosted by the response she got to her poem that she started writing poetry in a book at home and kept it up throughout the year, bringing the book in occasionally to show her work.

Animal poems

Then we had a book week at school on the theme of Animals. The whole school was asked to produce a display on this theme. So I chose to look at the theme of animals in captivity.

I pushed the desks back and chalked out an area at the front of the classroom. One after the other I put various children in the area and asked them to choose the animal they wanted to be and explain how they felt about their cage, or pool. I asked them to use the space as if it was their environment, and to explain what they were doing, feeling and thinking. After a few children had given us some examples, the class were invited to choose one animal (wild or tame) and put their feelings about captivity into a poem.

There was one boy in the class who constantly maintained a very negative stance about poetry, giving the impression he was too macho to write poems. He would, eventually, reluctantly, put a sentence down, cross it out, sigh and utter the exasperated cry of 'I can't do this miss!' The only way I could get him to continue was to talk through his ideas with him, questioning his responses and pulling out all the whys and wherefores. It was through doing this that I realised he had a lot of good ideas stored away. He decided to do a poem about his goldfish. We had read some poems about animals in captivity, and one had been about a goldfish, so I thought at first that he was just looking for an easy way out. But his poem proved to be very individual:

Goldfish

I'm so special he chose me . . . .
and the other three
we had a stormy journey home.
It isn't exactly the ocean,
and they feed me on paper,
But who am I to complain.
I'm special he chose me . . .
and the other three.

by Ryan

Elizabeth wanted to reflect the environment the whale lived in as part of the shape of her poem:

Why?

When I was born life was so
perfect compared to what I know
now
Why?
The fish so fresh and the ocean
so big
Why?
Then you took me away from my
home
Why?
You put me in a tiny tank and left
me there
Why?
People came and stared. They
banged on the glass and pulled
faces
Why?
I got ill. I couldn't do my tricks.
You all forgot about me.
Why?
I never asked you to take me
away.

by Elizabeth

55

Poem performances

One way of approaching poetry that really captured the children's imagination was performing it. We had looked at the work of four performance poets known as 'The Circus of Poets'. They were featured in a book called *Verse Universe* which accompanied a radio programme. We decided to use these poem performances as an assembly. In groups, the children chose one of the poems that they really liked. They sorted out backing music and sound effects. In art they made props, in drama they scripted the plays and practised performing them, and in English they decided to write their own performance poetry, on the theme of the playground, to be performed after the 'official' poems. They had such fun doing this that I made a mental note to include this activity earlier in the year, in future, and to give more time to it.

The Ball

Quick! Quick!
Catch the ball
Bouncing on the grass
Floating on the pond
Wherever it's going, it's going really fast!

Miss! Miss!
There's our ball
Bouncing on the grass.
Rolled in the pond.
Please let us in to get our ball.

When we picked the ball up, it was
Wet, slimy, cold and grimy
We don't want to play with it now!

by Charlene and Seeta

The Rush to the Playground

As the class is dismissed.
We run through the Hall.
Into the cloakroom
And down the stairs.
Pushing and shoving
'Cause it's a race

Out in the playground
Wet and damp
Joey Muddle is jumping in puddles
Zoe Cook is reading a book
Miss Carrot is shouting at Darren Parrot
"Stop that!"

Ding a ling a ling

The rush to the door
Up the stairs
Pushing and shoving
Into the cloakroom
Through the Hall
Into the classroom.

I won!

by Samantha and Naomi

As 'poetry appreciation' has now become a requirement for Year 6 SATs we also tackled this. It was another way of letting the class see the shape and the rhyming pattern of a poem and discuss the reasons why it had been made in this way. We did this as a whole class. There are many poems suitable for this, *Night Mail* by W H Auden, *Snake* by D H Lawrence and so on. The children really enjoyed sharing their thoughts and interpretations and acting like poetry detectives.

There are numerous ways of using poetry across the curriculum. Poetry can inspire art, and this is a fun way of looking at classical narrative poetry. Poems like *The Lady of Shalott* can be read aloud - then the children choose a verse to illustrate, and the poem and artwork are displayed together.

In history or PSHE (Personal and Social Health Education) poetry is the perfect medium for children to describe and express opinions and feelings without taking a 'comprehension exercise' approach. As a part of a 'people of vision' theme we were following in PSHE, we looked at the life of Harriet Tubman. We were able to spend time considering the details of her life and influence. In this way the children could understand more about the experience of slavery without coming at it in an abstract historical way. Some fine poems were written:

Caught

My dreams of Canada die away,
The dogs around me block my way.
All hope is gone. I'm full of fear.
The men on horse back are drawing near.
Their angry shouts ring in the air.
My heart is full of sad despair.
A terrible beating waits for me,
The country of Canada, I'll never see.

I'll be taken back to this life of pain,
I'll have to be a slave again.
I cannot bear the life ahead,
I wish just now, I could be dead.

by Gregory

Now I love poetry

Finally I asked the children to sum up how their attitude to poetry had developed over the year and choose their favourite poem from their year's work. This is what they said:

When I started writing poems I couldn't do it because I hadn't written poems before. The first time I had to write a poem I thought "NO WAY, I CAN'T DO THIS" but when I did write the poem it didn't rhyme so I started getting upset and grumpy because I thought my poem is going to be rubbish and everybody else's is going to be good but when I heard everyone else's poem, my poem sounded just the same but gradually I got better though my poems still don't rhyme. But that doesn't matter. I write poems without rhyming.

My favourite poem that I wrote this year was THE BALL.'
I chose this poem because I enjoyed working with my friend Seeta and exchanging ideas.
by Charlene

I used to be really stupid at poetry, I used to hate poetry. Now I love poetry. I've read other people's poetry. Some sad ones and sweet ones and rhymey ones and funny ones.
I try to write nice poetry. I love rhymey ones because they are like songs. If I am sad or unhappy, I am going to write poems that link with my mood.
I think poetry is a really nice thing because when you are bored you can read poems to cheer you up.
I hope in future more people will like poems.
My favourite poem that I wrote is:

The Gorilla Behind Bars

He was in the wild,
Happy and really mild.
Now in his cage.
Mad with rage.

The dark fur.
His eyes a blur.
Tears in his eyes,
He cries.

Wrapped in his thoughts of sadness,
Screaming with madness.
He's losing his hair,
But people don't care.

What is the meaning?
He does have feelings.

Susie Yao

The Gorilla Behind Bars

He was in the wild,

Happy and really mild.

Now in his cage,

Mad with rage.

The dark fur,

His eyes a blur.

Tears in his eyes,

He cries.

Wrapped in his thoughts of
sadness,

Screaming with madness.

He's losing his hair.

But people don't care.

What is the meaning?

He does have feelings.

*I like it because I love animals but I hate
them being ill treated. I hope when people
read this poem they would think twice
about hurting animals.*
by Susie

*When I first started poetry I didn't really
understand it. It was quite boring. I
thought poems had to rhyme. But
eventually I realised after reading poems
with the class I found it didn't have to
rhyme and I knew how to write a poem.
When I wrote rhyming poems they didn't
make sense. (I was trying so hard to make
it rhyme, I forgot what I was writing, but
now when I write rhyming poems they do
make sense). Mrs Maguire I think really
made it sound quite easy and now I
understand a little bit better. I chose a
poem about my sister because it is funny.*

This poem is about my sister

My sister has a big fat belly,

Who likes to eat a lot of jelly,

And when she finds out what I
have wrote,

She'll get a knife and cut my
throat,

And I'll say it wasn't me,

And that will be the end of me.

by Hollie

The greatest reward from the year for
me was seeing the obvious enjoyment
the children got from reading and
writing poetry, the growing
confidence in their own ability, and the
generosity of spirit that went with the
sharing of everyone's work. It proved
to be one of the few areas of the
curriculum where everyone achieved
and also gained respect in the eyes of
their fellow pupils.

Maria Maguire
Southfield Primary School
London Borough of Ealing

Children Performing Poetry

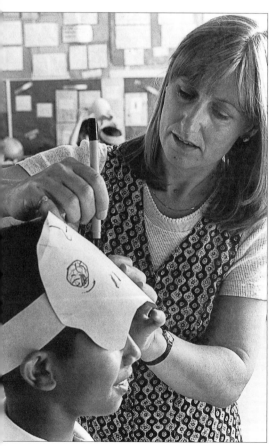

Linda Mariani

I was interested to raise the level of performance of the children in my class who, whilst mostly very fluent readers, were not confident at performing either their own work or the work of published poets.

We started by having a wealth of poetry in the classroom. Some resources belonged to the school and were gleaned from all over the building, but the majority of books belonged to me, having been collected over many years, for different age groups I had taught, and for my own enjoyment.

A regular time was set aside each week for poetry, which became part of our writers' workshop. This was a time when the children knew they could bring in poetry books of their own, or poems they had written, to share with the class. The class also began to anticipate that at this session I would introduce a new poem, as well as bringing back an established favourite. We would write poems during this time as well. I include myself here, because I always tried to write along with the children and show them the stages that they needed to go through before accepting their own work as finished. One of the things they found toughest about poetry was amending what they were doing, and developing the poem through several different drafts until they were fully satisfied.

There was great interest in the poetry from the start and some poems instantly became firm favourites. These included poems by Grace Nichols from *Come On into My Tropical Garden* and *Can I Buy a Slice of Sky*.

Another favourite was *Quick Let's Get Out of Here* by Michael Rosen. These two authors are very different in style and this led to some discussion as to how their poems should be read. The children made comments such as 'this poem needs reading in a calm, soft voice...' or 'you have to speak for the different characters . . . '.

The children were very enthusiastic about hearing poems and having a go at writing, but still quite reticent about reading aloud. Some were happy to read their own poems; others didn't want anybody to see or hear what they had done! Mostly they wanted me to read their work aloud for them - which at this stage I was happy to do.

During the autumn term I had a final year student taking my class for ten weeks. This gave me the opportunity to visit other classes and work with them on reading and performing. The first class I did this with was a parallel age group to my own, who had had very little input with poetry. With very few exceptions, they were reluctant writers and readers. We chose to do some work around an old favourite from *Don't Put Mustard in the Custard* by Michael Rosen, a poem called *Down behind the Dustbin*. This is a four line poem where the second and fourth lines rhyme. We read the poem and then did our own version called *Deep down under water*. Rampant plagiarism! The children were very enthusiastic. One of my personal favourites was:

> Deep down under water
> I met a squid called Mick,
> I said 'do you like seaweed?'
> it said 'no it makes me sick!'

by Ben

Most of the children contributed, and the end product was a book which they shared with younger children. The class teacher informs me that it is one of the class's favourite books, as is evident from its dog-eared state!

Descriptions and riddles

Back with my own class in the spring term, by way of an introduction into descriptive writing we worked on poems describing various objects. The children were split into groups and each group was given a different object to work with: an open box of tissues, a large pair of dressmaking scissors, a fine rollertip pen, a small tape recorder

Each group was given a large sheet of sugar paper and they were invited to 'brainstorm' their ideas. The level of interest was very high and the descriptions that came out were extraordinarily detailed. The group examining the pen pulled out all the stops and came up with a list of over fifty words and phrases.

I intervened and offered suggestions for synonyms for words like 'hard' 'soft' and 'smooth'. The children fed back their lists of words and phrases to the rest of the class and then went on to create a poem. Many chose to work on their own. I suggested that maybe it would be simpler to concentrate on just one aspect of the object they were focusing on - its appearance, or its use:

Like an animal
it's shiny
black and hard.
the wire is like its tail
its ridges are like ears
the plug is like a spiky knob
on the edge of its tail.
(Tape Recorder)

by Sadiq

Small but useful
a long
cylinder shape.
smooth at the bottom
rough at the top.
blue all over
with orange writing.
click when you close it.
with tooth marks in the lid.
pointing on the paper
and then words appear.
(Pen)

by Iyesha and Lauren

These poems were read to other children as riddles, and they were invited to solve them.

Rap poems

By now the need for some urgent action was evident as the children were still shy of performing and tended to read in a very self-conscious fashion. Fortunately salvation was at hand as one of the children had come across the *Baby-K Rap Rhyme* by Grace Nichols in *Can I Buy a Slice of Sky*. He particularly liked the refrain and it seemed like an excellent way to

develop a sense of rhythm and performance. There were opportunities for introducing music as well.

I liaised with the teacher with responsibility for music in the school and we worked together for three sessions to develop four-bar rhythms. The children worked in groups and had to use a variety of instruments - as well as body parts(!) to make as many different sounds as possible.

After much hard work from all we finally settled on the use of one instrument to keep the rhythm going (a beating block), and to combine it with a cymbal and a tambourine. The children clicked their fingers during the refrain.

The end result was glorious melee of children having great fun. I recorded it on tape and at the end the children burst out into spontaneous laughter which I kept on the recording! The tape is now played frequently. The children performed the poem to the whole school and were very well received. Even five months later they could recall most of the poem. The most satisfying part of this was that children of all abilities were able to take part. For a class of not very cooperative children, this was cooperation at its best!

rhythms to help them tune into the activity. By the end of the morning we had a twelve-verse rap, with more than one style, but in which all the styles were complementary. Two groups who had not worked together came up with very similar raps, and these became our first and last verses. Here is an extract from the poem, which is known as the *Longshaw Rap*:

No more teachers
no more school
no more lessons
after all

We're sitting in our classroom
with our teddy bear
our teacher doesn't like us
so be aware!

We're playing in the playground
with our ball
a boy comes along
and kicks it out of school.

We're sitting in the classroom
reading a book
miss comes over
and says 'let's look'

No more teachers
no more school
no more lessons
that's what's cool!

The Longshaw Rap

Rap poems became the way of life after this and we decided it was time for us to have a go at doing our own. An opportunity presented itself very soon, when due to a variety of difficulties I suddenly found myself looking after two classes for a whole morning - my own plus a Year 2/3 (my own class from the previous year).

Here was a godsend! Down to the hall we all trooped as the classroom is not big enough for two classes. Firstly my class performed their *Baby-K Rap*, then they had to teach it to the other class, and then it was performed by both classes together. After that, in groups, the children were given the task of creating a rap about some aspect of school - we discussed what they might include. We also clapped out different

Presenting a topic through poetry

The need to perform our own work presented itself again at the start of the summer term. Our current class topic was 'the structure of the body' and we decided to make a performance poem as a way of presenting the term's work to the children's parents.

Initially I divided the children into groups of about four or five. Each group was allowed to choose and draw a body part and then brainstorm a list of all their ideas as to the function of that part of the body. This list was written on the same paper as their sketch.

The second stage of this process was to design a presentation which would enable all these different brainstormed ideas to be put together. We decided to use a cumulative format, as in *This is the House that Jack Built*. We ended up with several descriptive sections. Here are two:

> This is the head
>
> That nods
>
> And talks
>
> And eats all day
>
> And can wear a hat.

> This is the spine
>
> That's long and straight,
>
> With lots of bones
>
> And discs and bumps
>
> That bend
>
> And stretches
>
> And has shivers down it.

Once we had cracked this, the rest was easy and everything fell into place. The introduction to the whole poem was based on the beginning to *Funnybones* by Allan Ahlberg. From these beginnings we developed a fifteen minute piece which the children performed.

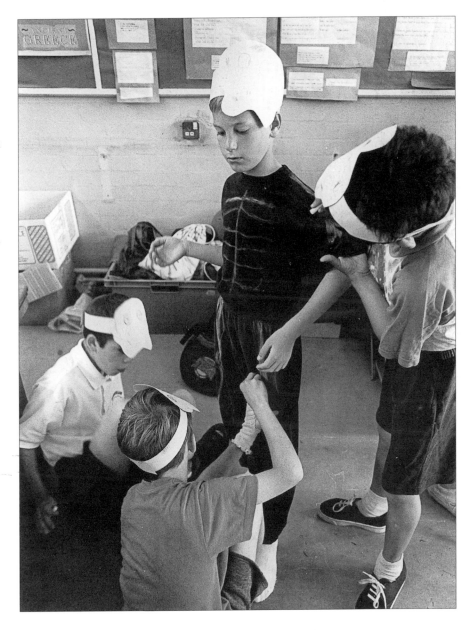

The performance

When the curtains opened (after some scene-setting with eerie music), the children were discovered sitting in a semi-circle around three sides of the stage. They lifted their heads, revealing skull masks, and chanted: *'On a dark, dark hill, there's a dark, dark town . . . some skeletons lived.'* Then they launched into their own poem:

> Skeletons, skeletons
> Come out at night
> Skeletons, skeletons
> Give you a fright!

While this was chanted, several of the pupils in skeleton costumes danced around the stage, until they were interrupted by a pupil who insisted that skeletons were *not* just about scaring people - there were lots of interesting things to learn about bodies and skeletons.

The skeletons sloped disappointedly back to their places and in turn each group of children stepped forward to recite their 'body parts' verses. Interspersed through the verses were occasional announcements about 'body facts'. Dances and movement were also used to create a visual and informative as well as entertaining fifteen minutes.

The performance ended as it had started with the children back in their semi-circle, with their skull masks on, reciting our own words to *Funnybones* - facts were okay, but it was more fun to scare people!

In a dark, dark school.
There's a dark, dark corridor.
Down the dark, dark corridor,
There's a dark, dark hall.
In the dark, dark hall,
There's a dark, dark stage.
And on the dark, dark stage
Some skeletons lived!

The whole performance lasted only fifteen minutes but it moved at a tremendous pace and every child performed with remarkable confidence. From comments received from the parents, staff and other pupils I knew it had been an impressive performance, and the progress made throughout the year was very evident. It was a great step forward for the class, who now have quite enough confidence to perform poems, whether their own or someone else's.

Linda Mariani
Longshaw Primary School
London Borough of Waltham Forest

Be a poet

'I brought hidden in a covered basket a gaily painted cockatoo, a carrot and a piece of gay ribbon.
"Why have you brought in these things?" asked the children. "Choose one thing, look at it, and write whatever comes into your head" I replied.
(Free Writing. Dora Pym, LUP, 1956)

In this chapter, I shall attempt to describe some of the activities that make up a writing workshop which I have been running in both primary and secondary schools over the past year, and on residential courses and summer schools for children of all ages. The workshop runs for a whole day and is informal, with the emphasis on enjoyment. In order to try out as many different activities as possible during the day, writing is not neatly copied out as it would be in a normal school environment and is left mostly, due to the confines of time, as 'work in progress'.

9.05am Surreal Consequences

This works well as a warm-up activity in that it is unusual AND involves the children writing in small groups on 'collaborative' poems; therefore, they can immediately get to know each other (if they don't already!) and don't need to feel that immediate pressure of having to 'perform' individually.

The writing game is one 'invented' by the Parisian surrealists of the 1930s and works in a way very similar to the parlour game 'consequences'. I talk a little about surrealism, especially the importance of 'dreaminess' then show

the children a five minute clip from the Hitchcock film *Spellbound* where a surreal dream has been 'filmed', the set of which was designed by Dali himself. There are houses with trees for chimneys, people running backwards down pyramids. . . . inspiring stuff. It stirs a good discussion about the 'strangeness of things'.

Now the children get into groups of about five and each child writes a line of poetry on a piece of plain paper. This can be quite spontaneous, often the first thoughts are the freshest;

'The twilight girl is dancing, dancing over the hills, away

(Susie)
or,
'She sat in the pond, a river of duckweed'

(Alice)
or,
'The sun beat down on the girl's flip flops'

(Melissa)

When all the children have written something, they pass the papers round in the same direction within each group. Now I ask them to write a fresh line of poetry which is the 'opposite' of what is already on the paper. This, of course, is a slightly 'mad' request but after an example or two, they soon get into the hang of things. (I remember once enraging my own junior teacher by writing in a futile grammar exercise

Jimmy Symonds

that the opposite of black was blue with pink spots. . .). The most important thing is that the children are made to feel confident enough to realise that what they write cannot be wrong.

So, the opposite of 'the queen danced softly in the meadow' might become 'a spaceman waved strangely in a field of turnips' or 'my auntie jumped over a sea of lionesses'. As in Consequences, the first line is now folded back before the papers are swapped for the second time, so it is useful to remind the children to leave a space of, say, 'two KitKats' between each line. They now repeat this activity until the papers have been all round the group. Of course, it doesn't have to stop there but often the children are excited to see what has been written. The papers are opened and a 'suitable' title is chosen for each poem. As the activity is played in the manner of a game, the children are often surprised by the 'poetic' result:

Crisps, hiss and squeeze
The crispy leaves of autumn
crackled under my footsteps
ruining my stealthy hunt creep
The fresh berries of Spring hissed
under my teeth
The over-ripe bananas of the
summer squeezed between my
fingers
The people who work in the zoo
are beginning to
squeeze like the animals do.

by Geoff, Alice, Alison, Amy

There are all sorts of possible interesting follow-ups to this activity. One is to quickly photocopy the papers and allow the children to make poetry collages by cutting up all the available lines of poetry, like a poetry bank. The completed poems can then be glued onto fresh paper and re-photocopied. It can even be interesting to cut up the lines individually, throw them in the air, then arrange them in a new pattern as they landed. it is a good introduction to 'accidental' artiness. I often tell the children the story of the film *If*, where there is one short sequence in black and white, the rest being in colour. Critics acclaimed this as being 'symbolic' at the time; when it was simply because the director had run out of cash!

11.17am . . . . Paperback Writer

This activity is 'inspired' by the story of the Lennon and McCartney song. Apparently, the Beatles were staying in a New York hotel (as pop stars do) and one said to another *'Close your eyes, spin around, open your eyes and write a song about the first thing you see'*. This was Ringo Starr in the bath, reading a paperback book. I might start this activity by playing the song.

I give the children a piece of plain paper and say something like this; 'I'm going to close my eyes, spin round and when I open them I'm going to pick up the first object I see. It might be anything. I want you to write or draw anything that comes into your head when you see the object. Keep writing, even if it's the same thing over and over again because that might help you think of a surprising thing, rather like when you make a row of dominoes and flick the first one and all others come tumbling down. Ready. I'm closing my eyes. Steady. I'm spinning. Go!'

There's always 'something' in a room. I try and choose something slightly strange, but even a pair of school round-edged scissors can become, in the imagination of an excited child, a pair of siamese twins or a stick insect feeding on two coconuts. I move the object around the room freely so the children can see it from as many different perspectives as possible, and also because they find it fun. At the end of the time, they share with the others what they wrote. Here are Susie's responses to a piece of gnarled wood;

- Pepper, my gerbil
- Christmas at Grandma's
- our conker tree
- being scared of spiders
- being accused of something I didn't do
- Smurf (the cat) catching a mouse
- fight at school
- Salt, my other gerbil
- my old house
- 'don't touch the ground' on the conker tree
- thunderstorm when we were out raspberrying and nearly got struck by lightning

This is a poem in itself but I suggest to the children that they use the page of writing as a 'sketch book' of possible ideas and develop just one of them. Susie decides to choose Pepper the gerbil as the starting point for a poem and writes this;

My Gerbil

Pepper is dead.
She died from a disease.
Horrible.
I can remember
When she lay cold and stiff
After weeks of silent suffering.

Pepper has a grave.
It's in a corner of the orchard.
Beautiful.
Her grave
Is surrounded by snowdrops.

Here is another poem written as a result of this activity:

Scissors

Mother's cutting up material.

She sees scissors, I don't.

I see Siamese twins, trying to escape and run from each other.

Mother sees scissors, I don't.

I see Mother and child back to back, standing as part of one another, lovingly.

Mother sees scissors, I don't.

I see a toucan, beak and all, eyes peering, glaring at me viciously.

Mother sees scissors, I don't.

I see a palm leaf, hanging beneath two coconuts, a small insect searching upon it.

Mother sees scissors, I don't.

by Ann

It often helps to concentrate the creativity of children to give them a limited amount of time to complete their poems, say four minutes and seventeen seconds (even though you might secretly let them have longer). They respond to the challenge and can feel great pride in achieving so much in so short a time, especially as it took Wordsworth about ten years to complete *The Prelude!*

2.25pm . . .Proustian Smarties

This is a good activity to reserve until after lunch because it involves eating lots of sweets. It's quite good fun to show children a copy of Proust's masterpiece because it's such an enormous book and obviously children are amazed by the scale of things. The link between the novel and the activity is rather far-fetched, except that it is the eating of little Madeleine sponges in a Paris cafe that provides the novel with some of its most beautiful passages, connected with idyllic memories. This activity follows on neatly from the previous one in that it is all about taste (and the colour of food) stirring the memories and thoughts of children.

Some sweets work better than others. For instance, in my experience Polos aren't as inspirational as Extra Strong Mints, and ordinary chocolate, however delicious, doesn't stir the imagination of a child as much as something interesting with chocolate inside it, such as Smarties. Smarties are tremendous and all the different colours create a good structure for poetry. In this activity, I gave the children six different coloured Smarties and told them they could present the writing as they wished. Here is Alison's result:

GREEN
The weekend I went away and ate cabbage for the first time.
Grass topped with snow.
ORANGE
A bright, glowing warm sun.
Hard mud turning to soft mud.
Snail shells crunched to the snail.
BLUE
The vast area of water of the world.
The water washed away to sand.
RED
A ball of fire and flame.
The sunset at night.
BROWN
My wormy that drowned.
The earth at night.
YELLOW
The slug I trod on when slime came out.
A cockerel crowing.

Alison decided to leave her writing in 'sketch book' form but Michael decided to develop one idea (the word 'Eldros') into a short story, having eaten a green Opal Fruit.

Eldros

The water was cold and refreshing. And yet he struggled against it, and the struggle exhausted him. And he felt heavy. He had eaten such a lot! But it had been the greatest wedding since that of Eldros. Especially after these long years of war. He climbed onto the banks of the river En and sat there, breathing heavily. And he went to sleep.

It was there that the newly weds found him. They gently carried him to Berthal and they slept there too. They all dreamt about their wonderful feast, because it was still fresh in their memory. And thus ended the most wonderful day in the history of Eastworld that lies beneath the stars of Agnes.

In the classroom, the children could suggest a different sweet each week, making a class book of poetry inspired by sweets, or fruit, vegetables, even Madeleine sponges!

Conclusion

These are just three of the many activities I have tried with children, some with more success than others. I have recently started to write with the children during each activity so that when we share what we have written, I also have to read out my attempts, which can be very embarrassing but I think it is ridiculous for a teacher to expect a child to do something which he hasn't tried himself.

My aim in preparing workshop activities is that the children shouldn't feel that they are working, but more that they are playing. I feel that it is in the fun, playful environment that I try to create, that children of all ages can produce their most creative writing.

Jimmy Symonds

Organising a Poetry Week

Varina Emblen

During the Spring term of each year we organise a literary event for the whole school to enjoy. In October of the year of the CLPE poetry workshop, I discussed with the staff the idea of a poetry week. They were interested, but worried about what they would have to do. Their anxieties seemed to stem from their lack of knowledge about poetry and their apprehension about teaching it. We had many discussions during which the following reasons for holding a poetry week were agreed on:

- to raise awareness of poetry among children, teachers and adults in the school community
- to read new material and revisit old favourites
- to hear what poets have to say about writing poetry
- to celebrate poetry in a variety of cultures, languages and styles.

I had kept a large selection of children's poems from previous years and we prepared for the week by discussing children's poetry. We had several meetings about how different results were achieved and about the range of formats that poetry could take. The resources that were most popular with teachers were all of the books written by Sandy Brownjohn and *Catapults and Kingfishers* by Pie Corbett and Brian Moses. These were widely used by staff in the run-up to Poetry Week and all samples of children's work were kept.

Meanwhile I began gathering a large collection of poetry from around the school. I gathered into one central collection all of the poetry books from classrooms, from the library and from book areas around the school. I had previously bought, from the commission earned on book fairs held in the school, a large selection of poetry books, and had kept these new books out of circulation. They were now added to this central collection. I spent further money from my English curriculum budget on a range of poetry books to cater for the interests of the children in our school (who range in age from three to eleven years). The whole, by now large, collection was stored away until one month before Poetry Week started, when it was presented to the staff. The books were displayed prominently in classrooms and teachers read poetry to children at least once a day in the run-up to poetry week. The books were given a very special status by class teachers.

During the Autumn term I had contacted the Children's Discovery Centre (also known as Bookspread) in Tooting, which will organise all the contacts you need to run a Book or Poetry Week. The bookshop staff advised me of poets who would visit schools and Brian Moses and Wes Magee both agreed to come. All I had to do was contact these poets to arrange an itinerary for the day of their visit. Their programmes consisted of workshop sessions and performances to larger groups. Michael Rosen, whose workshop I was attending regularly, also agreed to come and perform his poetry for all the children in KS2.

A week before

A week before the event, preparations really started. Parents were told by letter of the Poetry Week and of the days when poets would be in school. Also at this time, children were told that if they could learn any poem off by heart and recite it without any hesitations, then they could be videoed, either in groups or individually.

A Poetry Tree was constructed in the hall. Green leaves were cut out and put in a basket at the bottom of the tree and children were encouraged to take a leaf and write their favourite poem on it. The leaves were then stuck on the branches for all to read.

Throughout the previous year, as I already mentioned, I had been collecting examples of children's own poetry. These were now mounted, and poems written by children during the current year were added to the collection. As teachers had been focussing on writing poetry during the run up to this week, there was quite a lot of work to collect. One night after school we covered every noticeboard and wall in all the communal areas of the school with this collection - Penwortham is a large three storey building and the whole place was now covered with children's poems.

When the children came in the next morning there was lots of discussion about this huge exhibition! The display also got the parents involved, and we set up a large board where poems in other languages could be displayed. Children brought these poems into school, and we soon had a collection of poems in over twenty languages.

The Headteacher collected a copy of their favourite poem from every member of staff, and these were put into a book which was left near the main office for visitors, children and parents to read. In classrooms, as well as reading aloud, learning off by heart, and writing on the leaves of the poetry tree, children were encouraged to choose their favourite poem to be laminated. These mounted and laminated collections were made into individual booklets, each with title and author and the name of the child who had chosen it on the front. This method of presenting poems was adopted by all the class teachers and each corner of the school now had a collection of favourite poems. It made the poems much more accessible to the children as they did not have to wade through a whole book to find a poem that would instantly appeal to them.

The Section 11 team gathered together a collection of skipping and clapping rhymes in a variety of languages. Parents were asked if they would write out traditional rhymes for children, which they willingly did. These, too, were mounted on a display board near the main entrance for all to read and became quite a talking point among parents and children alike. In the playground, children were learning skipping and clapping rhymes in a wide range of languages.

There was now poetry activity going on all round the school. Children were practising feverishly for their video performances. In the playground, there were groups of children dancing to their favourite rap poems. In the classrooms, children were poring over books, 'testing' each other to see how well they could recite their chosen poem, and often hiding books around the classroom so that nobody else would choose the same poem to learn! Because of the massive interest that had now been generated, the children were very keen to take the books home. As we really wanted this enthusiasm to reach out to the wider school community, we decided to allow the poetry collections home with the children as part of the PACT scheme, on a one-night only loan.

Launching Poetry Week

Poetry Week was launched on Monday with a visit to the school by Brian Moses. He read to the children and performed a range of poetry using instruments and even dance. He also worked with class-sized groups on starting points and ideas for poems, as well as looking at the range of formats that a poem can take. The rap poetry he used was particularly popular. People were now becoming excited! There were interesting discussions in the staff room about the tremendous range of poetry in the class collections, and about the enthusiasm with which the children were reading them. These collections had demonstrated to children and teachers alike that boundaries had been broken down and that a poem could be many things.

As well as rediscovering old favourites, everyone was being introduced to a huge range of new works. Many teachers were amazed at the variety and quality of the poetry and could see many ideas that they could use in their own teaching. Children were seen to be enjoying a wider range of poetry, not just the jokey witty poetry they all love, but more thoughtful and serious poems. They were being given access to difficult language structures and ideas, as well as learning to use their everyday language and experiences in poetry. They were ready to listen to more complex poetry and to read and talk about it. A poetry culture had been established by all the work that had gone on in the school prior to the week itself.

The key to the children's successes as poets seemed to stem from the fact that they were being exposed to poetry. They could read it everywhere, in the classrooms, in books, on cards, in each other's work, even on the walls of the building they were in. They were hearing poetry read to them by teachers, children, family members and poets. They were seeing it performed in assembly by other children and by poets visiting the school. The confidence to have a go was evident in every classroom.

Poetry Week continued with performances in the hall from children, readings by teachers and children, and a visit from Wes Magee. His style of delivery and his quiet, humorous approach were quite different from the performances of Brian Moses on the day before. Wes had a great rapport with the children and the classroom workshops he gave were very successful and productive. These sessions were also very helpful to teaching staff who were able to use many of the ideas in their teaching.

Assemblies were totally devoted to poetry this week and as the children became more and more exposed to poetry so their enthusiasm grew. Children performed poems to the school as individual recitals, class groups, and singing and dancing groups. Poetry Week was due to be concluded by a visit from Michael Rosen, with a performance to the whole of Key Stage 2. From this riotous performance we wrote a collection of ideas into two poems beginning with the words:

> Down by the dustbin
> I met a dog called Jim
> He didn't know me
> And I didn't know him . . .

and . . .

> Do you know what
> Said jumping Jim
> I had a bellyache
> and now it's gone . . .

We went round the class and added our own verses to these beginnings and came up with our own versions which were made into books.

Another area touched on by Michael's performance was that of sibling rivalry. This was a rich subject that I resolved to investigate further at a later date with my class of Year 6 children.

Poetry Week had been due to conclude with the visit by Michael, but so much work was now under way in classrooms that the staff wanted the focus to continue for another week. I was thrilled with the fantastic response the week had generated and I suggested that we devote a staff meeting to a 'Show and Tell' session where we could see some of the things that had been happening in each other's classrooms, and share some of the children's work. This was very productive and gave us a host of ideas to use.

Poetry with Year 6

In my own classroom we had been reading and listening to a variety of Rap poetry and the class were keen to use musical instruments in performing these poems, as Brian Moses had done when he performed. We talked about the sort of things they could write about in a rap and came up with a list including: shopping, keeping safe, bullies, bad boys, dancing etc. I read a collection of poems by Lorraine Simeon and some from a collection called *Come Rock With I* edited by Morag Styles, as well as the class favourite *Curtis the Hip Hop Cat*. We talked about the constituents of a rap and the class agreed that the poem must have rhythm and rhyme.

The class sorted themselves into groups, but needed a tremendous amount of teacher help to get them going. I had taken for granted a knowledge of rhythm and rhyme that several children did not have. We

brainstormed lists of the vocabulary around their chosen themes and looked at words that would go together. Once the first two lines of a poem were in place they seemed to get the idea and were able to follow with their contributions. Working in groups definitely helped, as they were bouncing ideas off each other.

As the children wrote, they used large pieces of sugar paper and wide felt tipped pens; the whole poem was a group effort. When they were happy with the result the children set about practising performing the poem and added music and sound effects. Some of the boys wanted to dance too, so we practised this in the classroom.

The 'Shopping Rap' came from the idea of always being dragged round Sainsburys on a Friday night. The boys in this group felt that they didn't really need to be there but were forced to go along to help carry the bags or take charge of younger brothers or sisters.

The boys were unwilling to redraft too much of the poem and consequently it still has a 'list' quality about it. However the performance was stunning as they danced and played instruments to accompany the poem.

The Shopping Rap

I hate shopping because it
drives me mad!

The crisps are nasty and they
taste real bad.

I go with my mum and her
name is Polly

She's a real bad sport she won't
let me use the trolley.

I go down the aisles and I drop
all the packets

My mum gets cross and makes
a big racket

I begged my dad for an orange
lolly

He said "Go and ask your mum
Miss Polly".

I feel hungry in the long long,
long queue

I wish those Jelly Babies I could
chew

We pick up our bags, mum Polly
makes a fuss,

Don't know where we're going
to queue for the bus

We were standing on the bus
when the shopping bag snapped
That's why we sing the shopping
rap!

*by Lloyd, Fawwad, Gregory and
Toby*

The 'Bad Boys Rap' began with a list of
things that bad boys would do, such
as spoil others' games, not take turns,
misbehave in class, and so on. Once
they had the idea of the content , the
group worked well. After practising it,
they dressed up and shouted their
poem in a memorable performance.

Bad Boys Rap

Now this is the rap of the three
bad boys

We like to mash up little kids'
toys.

Out in the playground when we
play cricket

We push them off the crease
and smash up the wicket.

We run outside and grab the bat

We're supposed to take turns
but we don't care about that.

When we play football we foul
real bad

And then the other team get
really mad

When we're back in class we're
meant to make a mask

Instead we just play about and
mess up the class.

We got told off by Mrs Hubble

Then we were in really deep
trouble

We were grounded for a week
and Dad took our toys,

So don't copy us we're the
three bad boys.

by Neil, Ahmed and Mohammed

The 'Playground Rap' was another rap
for voices, with the chorus being
chanted continuously in the
background. The girls who wrote it
began with the chorus or chant idea
('This is our playground, our
playground') and built the poem
around that. There was little written
down in the early stages as they
seemed to go straight into a dance
routine, redrafting orally. They were
then encouraged to write as they went
and made a few alterations. They
performed the rap with a dance
routine and used instruments to
accompany their performance.

The rhyming couplet form of rap
poetry was very popular with Harriet
and was a form that she had used
many times before. An avid reader,
Harriet had a wide range of vocabulary
at her fingertips. She wrote another
dancing rap, and Jay danced and
performed her poem to the school:

Dancing Girl

I'm a dancing girl, I dance in the street,

I dance all day and I dance all night

I dance in the dark and I dance in the light

I dance in the morning when I'm eating my crumpet

I dance after school when I'm blowing my trumpet

I dance in the garden and I dance in the shed

I dance at home and I dance in bed

Wherever I go, whatever I do,

People are looking and so will you

I've danced everywhere, that's plain to see

I really have got the dancing key!

by Harriet

All these poems were completed within three days, from start to finished 'best' copy. All were performed to the school and a display was made of the written work. The children were very appreciative of each other's work and began to seek out more rap poetry. The rhyme was the thing that mattered: this seemed to be an important element throughout the term following this exercise. This kind of poetry seemed to have instant and universal appeal in my class.

As Poetry Week turned into Poetry Fortnight and eventually came to a conclusion we all declared it a great success. It had achieved everything we had set out to achieve and more. The influence on teaching poetry was very far reaching and we began to appreciate as a staff that *exposure* to poetry is the key to enjoying it, and being able to write it. We particularly noticed a new sense of corporate 'ownership' of poetry by children. Now they seemed to feel: this is something we all like, something we can all do and contribute to because we all have had experiences, and those experiences are valuable and can become 'poetry'.

Varina Emblen

Ways into English with bilingual children

Michele Rowe

I welcomed the opportunity to become involved with the year-long poetry group with Michael Rosen, particularly to develop poetry with bilingual children. For years I have been interested in watching closely how children, whilst learning English, move from using single words to simple phrases and observing how poetic in structure their expression often is.

For the past six years I have been teaching in an infants school in Tower Hamlets as both a class and a section 11 teacher, teaching children between the ages of three to seven years. Ninety eight percent of our children are bilingual, the majority of them from Bangladesh and at the very earliest stages of learning English. For most of the children, school is their first major experience of using English. As Sylheti, the predominately spoken dialect of our children, is only just developing as a written language, school also provides, for many children's families, their first experience of reading and writing. Many of the older children in the infants, as well as learning English, also learn Arabic and standard Bengali at Mosque and community schools, and are brought up in a multilingual environment.

I am fortunate to be bilingual myself, having learnt Dutch as my second language. I learnt this as an adult whilst living in Holland for ten years before I came to the U.K. Learning a second language has helped me to see what is involved for children in becoming bilingual.

Our School Fire

In February 1992 our school was completely demolished by a fire, and it was the outburst of work after this that showed me how poetic bilingual children's use of English can be. The childrens' work after the fire was precise in meaning yet lively and immediate.

I knew, from experiences of my own young son having watched the fire with me, the effect the fire would have on our young children. The image of billowing clouds of black smoke that were seen across London, flames escaping, stayed firmly imprinted on my retina for weeks. I knew how much this would mean for the children.

Here are some samples of some of the work that followed.

Warm Fire

Warm fire

and the glass is banging

The roof in the fire

All the things

banging . . . .

Transcribed from Shabul Age 6 (Along with Shabul's accompanying picture he wrote his first complete word 'fire')

The windows were banging

The door was open

The smoke was in the sky

The paper was burnt

The fire engine was coming

eeee aaaa eeee aaaa

The tidy boxes was broken

The crayons was burnt

The tap was broken

and the water splashed

The End

by Amina
(transcribed from her own
emergent writing)

Masima was looking at the
window

And the door was open

And the smoke was coming in
our door

Smell of fire

My cousins' windows were open

And they could smell it too

They thought the fire was in their
house

Coming up their chimney

by Masima
(Transcribed from her own
emergent writing)

Remembering this explosion of expression, I wanted to look at ways to spark children's emotions and feelings and maintain the vibrancy of this kind of expression. But simultaneously I also wanted to look at ways to develop the children's English and enrich their sense of language, without taking away too much from their intrinsically poetic form of expression.

Where to begin?

As an infant teacher developing children's English, where would I begin? Especially as I'd always felt (as many teachers do) a bit nervous about developing children's poetry. Michael encouraged us in the poetry group to reflect upon our own experiences of poetry at school and how this could affect our own anxieties and practice with teaching poetry. I could remember as a child reciting long verses by heart and feeling anxious about how to meet expectations of using metre and rhyme. At times I had felt desperate and inadequate. I gradually realised poetry need not necessarily be constrained by rhythm and rhyme, which for me had been overemphasised at school. Michael Rosen's 'nonsense' poetry seemed to be extending the usual definitions of poetry.

Throughout the duration of the poetry project I was working as a Section 11 support teacher with two Year 1 classes. In total sixty-one children were at the very earliest stages of learning English. To make the best use of our limited support we targeted children with the least English. Some were still in a 'silent phase', reluctant or unable to speak English.

I was able to work closely and plan with the two class teachers, who were enthusiastic about the poetry group and keen to explore different aspects of poetry. Throughout the year we were able to spark off and complement each other's ideas. We decided our topic for the Autumn Term would be 'Books and Nursery Rhymes'. As I was still a bit nervous I wanted to begin from a secure base.

The relationship between core books, rhythm, repetition and rhyme has been well researched, and it is surely this relationship to poetry that has made core books so popular. Books with strong repetition and rhythm are fun to read with children. They provide a structure that is easy for children to pick up and remember. For bilingual children this kind of structure is very important. Through their experience with books they are being introduced constantly to new words and language structures. Repetitive structures help them not only to hold on to new words but also to remember new forms of language.

Providing Structures

My focus on the issue of repetition and its relationship to poetry was encouraged when, during one of our workshop sessions, Michael asked us to write a poem about a typical breakfast time in our own households. We were encouraged to take ideas not only from what we saw but also from what we were thinking, feeling and hearing - a multi-sensory approach. Michael suggested we should further develop our first ideas, and experiment with repetition. We might choose to isolate one or two lines from our original poem and rewrite another version. The results of this exercise were fascinating, especially when we read the poems out loud within the group. The second versions were fuller, more amusing and more interesting to read, as well as having a stronger rhythm.

Michael gave us further ideas for developing children's poetry.

• *Repetition and noises*
Concentrating on noises heard, to develop repetitions around a particular theme: children add their own lines

i.e.   Splish splash

        Splish splash

as a refrain for a poem.

• *Poem cartoons or portraits*
Using drawings and developing dialogues between one or more people in a picture. Including in the poem what they are thinking, feeling, seeing or hearing as well as their actual words.

• *Snapshots*
Taking a 'snapshot' view of all the things happening and being said at any one time in a particular place, and compiling them together in a group poem (eg. in the playground, tidy-up time).

Each Peach Pear Plum

Meanwhile our theme within the class was already taking shape. Our first book was *Each Peach Pear Plum*. Despite its seeming simplicity, this book is extremely rich – not only does it highlight well known nursery rhymes and stories but it develops its own rhyme and rhythm with its own skilful plays on words and use of repetitive lines. The accompanying illustrations encourage children to look closely for hidden cues, which are further supported by a clever use of rhyme.

It has always struck me how quickly children learn and echo the rhythm as rhyme of this book, particularly bilingual children, who 'sing' its strong rhythmic pattern (*My Cat Likes to Hide in Boxes* is another book that has a similar effect). *Each Peach Pear Plum* was a perfect way for children to practise the sounds of English and play with rhythm and rhyme. To bring the characters and stories further to life we read the corresponding nursery rhymes and stories. We made story props, picture cards and word games to help build the story's sequential structure and aid recognition of words. As a maths activity we made a chart of the children's favourite characters. Our underlying aim was to develop a deeper understanding of the story and the characters as well as the rhythmical aspects of the book.

For the children we simplified and broke down the structure, making individual books with them which used the repetitive phrase 'I Spy'. Behind corresponding 'flap doors', the children drew or wrote their own characters.

To further develop 'I Spy' we did work around the senses. We used a song the children were learning *These Are My Eyes* as a basis for more individual books ('I can see' 'I can hear' 'I can feel') picking up on the structure of the song and its repetitions. But I wanted to take this a step further and use Michael's idea of 'picture poetry'.

We developed the sensory poetry further when we went on a walk to the park. We brainstormed the things that children expected to see and hear beforehand, then recapped this on our return, before the children began their work.

A Dark Dark Tale

Throughout the term we did more work using repetition and rhythm to explore books and emphasise story structures. *A Dark Dark Tale* always appeals to the children's sense of adventure and humour. Turning off the lights and darkening the room while reading it enhances the effect.

Again the children made their own flap books, this time in the form of a house. We simplified the book's repetitive phrases to make it easier for the children to hold onto its structures and rhythms. To bring out feelings of suspense and fear, we talked about things they were scared of, and suggested they use them in their work. Many 'dark,dark' poems resulted from this.

One of the children's sisters (a year 2 child) also brought in her own 'dark dark house' book to show me, and we shared this with the class:

A dark dark house

In the dark dark house

was a dark dark stairs

    stairs

  the

up

there was a dark dark door

Behind the dark dark door

there was a

skeleton

by Runa

A Dark Dark Tale was further developed in Art and Design and Technology, with the children creating dark, dark boxes to make and hide their own scary object. The scary theme had been so successful in sparking the childrens' imaginations we continued it and collected more 'Scary Books' such as *Knock, Knock Who's There* by Sally Grindley and *This is the Bear and the Scary Night* by Sarah Hayes.

Speaking with the heart

Michael encouraged us to work with other poets to explore and use other techniques to further develop our own styles and teaching. During the spring term I also enrolled myself to do three workshop sessions with Margot Henderson. This course was aptly titled *Speaking with the heart*. Margot works with a variety of techniques and resources:- clapping patterns, partner and circle games; pictures and artefacts to develop rhythm, playing with words and feelings and with different ways of developing description.

One kind of poetry we explored was around weather. Before writing we had some introductory activities to explore our feelings and associations with weather and to create an ambience. Again as a group we worked to create the sound of rain. Starting with one finger, then two fingers, building on the dynamics, from very quiet soft and gentle spitting rain building to a loud thundery explosion and then back down again. The feeling was electric - the scene was perfectly set for us now to write. This whole approach of providing introductory activities so that children need not go 'cold' into their writing is obviously very important.

Autumn Term

A new year has just begun and I am working with two new colleagues. I am working with the same two classes, who are now year 2. Being with the same children is great, we can continue where we left off. Our first topic is food and we have already made class and individual books from *The Very Hungry Caterpillar*. We've used it to begin science work on healthy and unhealthy foods - predicting, dissecting, and tasting food. With the targetted children we've made zig-zag books using the very hungry caterpillar as a starting point.

I want in future to move further into areas of developing poetry through rhythm and rhyme - to continue to use repetition but to develop these other elements too. I want to develop music more and link it to the practice I have developed this year as being part of the poetry group. And I want to move into making more use of word families, so as to keep poetry and playing with words alive.

Michele Rowe
Blue Gate Fields Infant School
London Borough of Tower Hamlets

Thank you to Michael Rosen and Myra Barrs for the project. To the group for the support. Thank you to my colleagues last year, Tessa Lloyd and Sara Pala. Thank you to Margot Henderson for her inspiration. And finally thank you to children from Moon and Mars classes (now Neptune and Mercury classes) at Blue Gate Fields Infants School, 1994/1995.

A year with poetry

As a piece of INSET, this one-year workshop was unique in my experience, and it was a particularly rare phenomenon in the current climate, when the majority of teachers' courses now have to be short and snappy, and the 'market economy' in professional development means that everything has to be paid for. Here was a chance for teachers to work with poetry for a whole year, with the support of a well-known writer and teacher in this field.

Prior experiences

Towards the end of the year I interviewed six of the ten teachers who had been involved in the group. I wanted to find out more about their impressions of the year and what they had learned from it. I asked them about their own prior experience of poetry, and of teaching poetry, and about how the workshop had influenced them. I asked them what it was about poetry that they felt made it a particularly important genre.

It was interesting to find out how many of those I interviewed said that they had been put off poetry either at school or at college. Poetry had seemed, in Varina's words, to be 'hard work - an object of study' . Colette remembered liking Spike Milligan at school, but being given a book by Charles Causley to read instead. Left on her own with this book, she had simply ignored it. Some people remembered no poetry at their primary schools at all. Teachers had sometimes made a difference and there were memories of one or two

'brilliant teachers' who had briefly made poetry come alive. Maria particularly remembered having taken to Wordsworth because of the enthusiasm of one of her sixth form teachers.

But the overall reaction to poetry had been that it was 'difficult'. Even at college, Jenny had responded to poetry mainly as an academic exercise - 'I never really felt it was talking to me.' Julia had recently found a college copy of T.S.Eliot, with the copious notes she had taken at the time running down all the margins. It had reminded her that this poetry had just passed her by; it was like reading a foreign language.

Positive influences

However, there had been some positive influences. Colette's father had been in the habit of saying Gujerati poetry to her and she had enjoyed these melodious sounds. ' It was the beauty that struck me; the words connected me to beautiful things'. Later, coming to Beowulf through her experience as a storyteller, she had particularly enjoyed the patterned language of the oral stories.

Similarly, Jenny had enjoyed meeting poetry as song (eg in the songs of *The Highwayman* and *The Walrus and Carpenter*) and as wordplay (especially in the work of the German poet Erich Fried), but at the time did not make a link between experiences of this kind and poetry 'proper'. In general, people had come to poetry late - Maria had done an A level English

Myra Barrs

evening course and, as part of this, read Keats and the metaphysical poets, when suddenly it 'all came alive'.

Sometimes the influences that had turned these teachers on to poetry had been personal. Julia had a friend and a sister who both read poetry and encouraged her to read it. On one occasion her sister had sent her a book by Wendy Cope as a birthday present - she reported herself as having been 'disappointed - but then enjoyed it'. Other influences came from the media. Varina particularly remembered a BBC2 Poetry Week, with Benjamin Zephaniah, which had introduced her to a different kind of poetry 'accessible and cosmopolitan. It just reached out and made me go and get the book'.

Joining the workshop

Before joining the workshop many teachers in the group felt that they lacked the confidence to teach poetry. They had tried working with poetry, with variable success. They particularly stressed the fact that they had little confidence in approaching the *writing* of poetry. Though they had sometimes worked out a way of teaching writing, drawing on resources such as Sandy Brownjohn's valuable books, they had not really made these approaches their own. In their own words, they were 'still stuck on a method'. Generally this method involved the heavy modelling of poetic forms; a poem being presented to children with the message 'look at this - now we're going to do one like it'.

Some felt that their lack of confidence

had rubbed off on the children. Julia felt that 'because I lacked inspiration perhaps the children did too'. Jenny came to realise that 'I was projecting my own fear onto them'.

I asked them to recall why they had wanted to join the workshop. Andrew said he had been 'uncertain how children write poetry - how you get them to do it.' Although he was reading a lot of poetry for children, and finding that it really worked in the classroom, he wanted to know more about how to develop the work. Maria, similarly, was used to using poetry with children and enjoyed both reading poetry aloud and getting children to write it. She had wanted to join the workshop to know more about this process. But a new class that she began to teach during the year of the workshop made her particularly anxious to take part. Suddenly, she realised that she had

always 'expected children to write straight away', but this new Year 6 class was very inexperienced in poetry and couldn't initially do what she expected of them.

Michele had been particularly interested in the workshop because of her role as a teacher of young bilingual children. She felt that repetition and rhythm meant a lot to young children. She remembered her own learning of Dutch, and the importance of imitating the intonation and tune of the language, and of hearing patterns and tunes. She wanted to use poetry as another way into learning English, a way that appealed to this strong instinct for pattern and structure in all learners.

The experience of the workshop

Attending the workshop was a daunting experience initially for several of those who stayed the whole course. Maria was frank about the fact that she 'started off terribly frightened and in awe. Every time somebody said something it sounded such a good idea. I was afraid I wasn't up to it'. Most people admitted that they had felt nervous in the early stages, and also somewhat awed at the prospect of working with Michael, as a 'celebrity'. Some were also concerned, in the first term, because they felt that change was not taking place rapidly enough. Colette was despondent: 'I felt I hadn't managed to go beyond what I'd done before'.

What was particularly useful to several group members early on was the opening up of definitions of 'poetry'. Michael had enlarged their ideas about what a poem could be, through a mixture of examples and writing activities. Gradually, through reading, talking, and playing with ideas for making poems, poetry came to seem a more accessible medium, and writing poetry a process that did not require special training. Jenny felt that the whole experience of these early meetings was 'freeing - language could be used flexibly! I loved Jackie Kay's poetry, with the Scottish dialect words'.

The workshop had been planned to include plenty of feedback from classrooms. Meetings settled into a pattern: we would often begin by writing ourselves (usually with a member of the group leading a writing workshop) and then tell about what had been happening in classrooms, showing examples of poems that children had been reading and writing. This pattern provided a wonderful context for picking up on other people's ideas. Julia felt that 'the informality of the setting helped - and the span of time that the workshop went on for. The spacing of meetings was good too - it gave us time to listen, try things out, and come back and tell about what had happened'.

As with all teachers' courses, one of the best features had been this sharing of teachers' practice. Everybody had enjoyed the opportunity to hear what others had been doing. Varina summed it up: 'There should be more sharing; teaching's so isolated'. And whereas INSET is often about hearing success stories, this long-running workshop enabled group members to share failures and problems as well as successes. Colette felt that 'the best thing was hearing how other people went through ups and downs - it was helpful to know that other people had the downs!'. Julia also underlined the importance of being able to make mistakes: 'If it had been slick presentations, perfect solutions, it wouldn't have helped so much. As the group gelled together they got better able to tell about the problems they were having. We all like to present a professional front - but there was none of that here. It was very supportive.'

In fact in the course of the year the members of the group had become very responsive to each another. For Maria, it had been 'very supportive, unassuming. It gave me tons of good ideas. It made me think why I was doing something and what I was asking of children.' Varina had found it 'helpful to see how others operate and from low-key starting points what they've achieved.' Andrew, reflecting on the value of attending courses in general, thought that 'it fuels interest in the job, it makes you reflect. I'd find it difficult to go on teaching day to day without constant injection of interest and enthusiasm such as this group gave.' For him, as for the others, 'it was wonderful working with Michael'.

Keeping a journal

Right at the beginning of the year Michael had stressed that being prepared to keep a journal was one of the essential criteria for inclusion in the workshop group. We knew we needed to capture the experience of the year and record the changes taking place. The journal was a difficult thing to keep going, but some group members found it made a real difference to their work during the year, making them 'remember more and listen more'. The journal helped them to look back over what they had done and build on it, and was particularly helpful as a way of recording and studying what children were doing. Varina reported that 'I've had a lot of surprises this year from children'. The journal had enabled her to actually analyse what children had done, how they'd done it, and what they knew - 'and they know a lot.'

For several people, as for Jenny, keeping the journal was part of the experience of the group and meant that 'the whole year I was thinking about poetry.' Newly alive to poetry, she began to read with a new interest the poems on the tube, which became 'almost like friends'. For Michele, the journal, like the workshop, provided a 'wonderful way of reflecting on one particular aspect of teaching for an entire year'.

Effects on pupils

I wanted to know how far they felt that these good professional experiences had been translated into positive experiences for children, and whether the teachers in the group felt that their classes had benefited from their participation in the workshop.

The teachers I interviewed were quite clear that there was now much more poetry - both reading and writing - going on in their classrooms. Children were approaching the writing of poetry with much greater ease, and appreciating each other's work. Andrew reported that he had had 'very sensitive poems from very unlikely children'.

Other teachers also confessed to being surprised with what the children in their classes had done. Maria emphasised that 'it is not just the bright kids, they are all capable - the most pleasing part of it was the effect on less able kids, and how proud they were of what they did'. In her class too, poetry had reached some unlikely children - one 'hard' boy, an army cadet, someone who just 'pushed poetry off', had written a really thoughtful and delicate poem.

Reading poetry had been particularly helpful, particularly poetry for children which was short and lyrical, almost like a snapshot. Poetry of this kind seemed a particularly available literary experience for children with literacy difficulties, it was 'a way of dealing with universal things, but in a flexible mode'. One child in Jenny's group had made 'incredible progress - initially imitating rhymes in pedestrian way and then moving into real poems, writing freely.' Jenny thought that working with tight structures at first may have given this child the confidence to go forward.

Several teachers had found that children actually responded to poetry more readily than to other forms of writing. Poetry reading had proved to be accessible to a wide range of children. Although initially they seemed to go mainly for quirky humorous verse, their tastes, and their range as writers, had developed when they were exposed to a wider choice of poetry. Varina quoted the case of one child who went 'from nothing to very strong poems - his confidence increased, he was suddenly prepared to use direct experience'. She felt that the key task the teacher had to do was to 'build the confidence in them to put down what they're thinking and feeling. I've seen the progression of all the children from September to now'.

How the teachers changed

There was a remarkable consensus among most of the teachers I talked to about how their practice had changed as a consequence of the workshop. Colette was clear about how the year's experience had affected her, saying 'Now I wouldn't put the method before the child'. Instead of looking for recipes and 'tips', she was putting more trust in reading poetry to children - 'reading from lots of different poets' work, reading a lot more'. She was finding that children picked up on these influences and that their repertoire was growing. Secondly, Colette was putting much more emphasis on personal experience as the material for poetry. The stress that Michael put on using real happenings and feelings as a basis for writing made sense to her. She was encouraging children to draw on their experiences and to record their thoughts and impressions in their poems. She found that this kind of approach had enabled more children to produce good poetry. Others agreed with her that this combination of being exposed to a great deal of poetry, and finding a personal subject matter, was what really counted. Looking back on her past practice, Julia said 'the fault was in trying to control the process too tightly'.

The group of teachers now felt far more confident and less inhibited about working with poetry. As Jenny observed: 'I feel I can teach the kids a lot better'. Like others in the group she had come to realise that 'there wasn't a right and wrong way of doing it'. The refined and polished kind of poetry that had been presented to her in formal education was not, she now saw, the only kind. And she was now able to trust her own interpretations and readings even of classic poems, having realised that poetry ' once it's written down is in the domain of the reader' . For her, there was now even something 'quite egalitarian about poetry. Each child has own voice, own way of speaking, way of seeing the world, and each way is valid'. The strong oral focus in poetry, that she enjoyed herself and that children she taught enjoyed, had been justified by her experiences during the year; she had got started by dipping a toe in water with cumulative rhymes and rhythms, and poems that were close to songs, and had progressed to free verse.

Most teachers stressed the central role that reading poetry aloud to children had increasingly come to play in their practice. Varina's account of this was one clear example; she had ' realised this year the importance of reading aloud at various points in the day. By surrounding children with poetry, you give them access to all sorts of structures, all sorts of models.' She felt that this created a 'poetry culture', a literate environment in which children and teacher could attempt more, and gradually take on quite difficult poetry. That was the 'method' she is

using now 'and it's far more effective than the old one'.

Maria had also started to read a lot more to children - including poems by children ('because I wanted them to know children could write'). In her classroom, poetry 'became all-encompassing - I've been using poetry in music, in drama, I've started to use it in history, in personal social and health education'. It had become a basic way of understanding experience, and of 'deepening knowledge', enabling children to identify more thoughtfully with the experiences of others. Maria was particularly concerned about the approach being adopted now in schools where poetry had become a 'blocked unit', with the school deciding to do poetry 'after half term'. This was, she thought, just awful. 'We should be doing it all the time'.

Why they value poetry

But, after all, is poetry really as crucial as this - and if so, why is it? I asked the teachers I interviewed to try to sum up what they felt to be so particularly important about poetry in education. For many of them, it was the scale of poetry which was so attractive and which made it so available to children.

'There's a sort of succinctness about it - a poem's something small and precious'. The special value of poetry, in Julia's words was that 'less can be more'. In a short space, a poem invites reflection, 'it helps you to dwell on things. And it's length makes it very available to the whole range of children in the class'.

Another major benefit of poetry, for many teachers, was the fact that it had shown children that they had something valuable to write about. 'It's good to make them realise that their experience counts', suggested Andrew. It was this ability of poetry to validate individual experience which had been particularly important for Varina. 'It crystallises their direct experience - really what's inside them - and is much more intense than other forms of expression. And everyone can contribute something. All the best things they've done have been direct experience.'

Maria also felt that poetry offered children a unique way of communicating. 'Because it's personal. It's very hard to be personal in a class. They matter - their experiences, their feelings, their thoughts. They can be appreciated. It's a way of sharing what's most intimate. They write about things they wouldn't talk about'.

In several classes, poetry had proved to be a help to children's reading development, providing them with a wide choice of short manageable texts which nevertheless extended them as readers. Andrew suggested that 'poetry develops a sensitivity to language, an enjoyment of words - and an awareness of the effect of words on people', and had noted improvements in children's reading as a consequence of their new interest in poetry. Jenny also valued the joy in language that poetry expresses, the playing around with words, which could involve all children, regardless of their perceived ability.

What next

All the teachers felt that they would continue to make poetry an important part of their teaching. 'I'd like to keep this pace up' said Varina. 'Because of writing the journal I've had to ensure that children were writing poetry at least once a month. After this year I'll do this always.' The people I talked to felt that it had been a good pressure to have to include poetry regularly in their planning. They wanted to promote these practices more widely within their schools, and put poetry more centrally on the agenda with their colleagues.

Individual teachers had different aspect of their practice that they wanted to develop. A number of them also wanted to further their own development. They were planning to take more poetry courses, perhaps to study poetry as part of an academic course, or to go to an Arvon writing workshop. This year's experiences had convinced them that they themselves could take a more confident part in reading and writing poetry.

Several teachers had resolved to read more poetry themselves, and had begun to find contemporary poets' work which spoke to them particularly strongly. (Margaret Atwood, Jackie Kay, Carol Ann Duffy and Adrian Mitchell) were mentioned). Michele had decided to do more work with music, picking up on the rhythmic structures in poetry which she found so important to children.

In general, teachers wanted to build on what had happened during the year, and on what they now knew worked for them and for the children in their classes. They wanted to provide more opportunities for children to read poetry, and to bring their personal experiences to their poetry writing. There was a new confidence about their approach; they felt that now they knew what they were doing in poetry. In the September of the year following the workshop, Maria was looking forward with anticipation to the prospect of teaching a new class of children whom she knew nothing about. 'It's like waiting for a flower to open', she said.

Julia looked back over the workshop year. She had come because she felt deficient in this area of her teaching and because she wanted help as a teacher, 'but actually it's been more like personal development'. Perhaps all real learning feels like that.

Myra Barrs

Bibliography

Children's books referred to in the text

John Agard: Lend Me Your Wings
Hodder & Stoughton 1987

John Agard: Say It Again Granny
Bodley Head 1986 Mammoth 1990

John Agard & Grace Nichols: No Hickory, No Dickory, No Dock
Viking 1991 Puffin 1992

Allan Ahlberg: Please Mrs Butler
Viking 1985 Puffin 1984

Janet and Allan Ahlberg: Each Peach Pear Plum
Viking 1984 Puffin 1989

Janet and Allan Ahlberg: Funnybones
Heinemann 1980 Mammoth 1990

Margaret Bateson-Hill: Lao Lao of Dragon Mountain
De Agostini 1996

Gerard Benson, Judith Chernaik and Cicely Herbert (editors): Poems on the Underground
Cassell 1996

James Berry: When I Dance
Hamish Hamilton 1988 Puffin 1990

Raymond Briggs: Fungus the Bogeyman
Hamish Hamilton 1977 Puffin 1990

Ruth Brown: A Dark Dark Tale
Andersen Press 1981 Red Fox 1992

Cadburys Books of Children's Poetry
Beaver - various dates

Eric Carle: The Very Hungry Caterpillar
Hamish Hamilton 1970 Puffin 1974

Faustin Charles: The Kiskadee Queen
Blackie 1991 Puffin 1994

Helen Cook & Morag Styles (editors): Come Rock with I
Cambridge University Press 1991

Helen Cook & Morag Styles (editors): Don't Do That!
Cambridge University Press 1991

Richard Edwards: The Midnight Party
Cambridge University Press 1993

John Foster/Korky Paul: Dragon Poems
Oxford University Press 1993

Sally Grindley/Anthony Browne: Knock Knock Who's There?
Hamish Hamilton 1985 Puffin 1995

Sarah Hayes/Helen Craig: This is the Bear and the Scary Night
Walker 1994

Susan Hill (editor): Poems Not to be Missed
Keystone 1991

Jackie Kay: Two's Company
Puffin 1992

Roger McGough: Pillow Talk
Viking 1990 Puffin 1992

Colin McNaughton: Who's Been Sleeping in My Porridge?
Walker 1990

Wes Magee: Witch's Brew
Cambridge University Press 1989

Grace Nichols (editor): Can I Buy a Slice of Sky?
Blackie 1991 Hodder Knight 1993

Grace Nichols: Come On into My Tropical Garden
A & C Black 1988 Lions 1993

Grace Nichols (editor): Poetry Jump-Up.
Puffin 1990

Gareth Owen: Song of the City
Collins 1987 Fontana Lions 1985

Brian Patten: Gargling with Jelly
Puffin 1986

Poetry Corner
BBC 1992

Michael Rosen/Quentin Blake: Don't Put Mustard in the Custard
Andre Deutsch 1996

Michael Rosen: Hairy Tales and Nursery Crimes
Lions 1987

Michael Rosen: The Hypnotiser
Andre Deutsch 1988

Michael Rosen/Quentin Blake: Quick Let's Get Out of Here
Puffin 1985

Dennis Saunders (editor): Hist Whist
Evans 1975

Lorraine Simeon: Stop That! an anti-bullying rap
Viking 1995

Eve Sutton/Lynley Dodd: My Cat Likes to Hide in Boxes
Spindlewood 1984 Puffin 1978

Alfred, Lord Tennyson/Charles Keeping: The Lady of Shalott
Oxford University Press 1989

Verse Universe
BBC 1992

Gini Wade: Curtis the Hip-Hop Cat
Macmillan 1986

Kit Wright/Peter Bailey: Tigerella
Andre Deutsch 1993 Hippo 1994

Benjamin Zephaniah: Talking Turkeys
Viking 1994 Puffin 1995

Teachers' books

Myra Barrs, Sue Ellis, Hilary Hester & Anne Thomas: The Primary Language Record Handbook for Teachers
CLPE 1988

Sandy Brownjohn: To Rhyme or Not to Rhyme
Hodder & Stoughton 1994

Aidan Chambers: Tell Me. Children, Reading and Talk
Thimble Press 1993

Pie Corbett & Brian Moses: Catapults and Kingfishers Oxford University Press 1986

Michael Rosen: Did I Hear You Write?
Andre Deutsch 1989

Helen Rosenthal: 'Introducing Poetry' in
Language Matters 1993/94 no 2, CLPE.

Poetry for children - a Core Booklist

KS 1

AGARD, John/Grace NICHOLS: No Hickory, No
Dickory, No Dock
Viking 1991 0670826618 Puffin 1992
0140340270

AHLBERG, Janet and Allan: Each Peach Pear
Plum
Viking 1984 0670287059 Puffin 1989
0140509194 Oliver & Boyd (Big Book)
0050044060

BENJAMIN, Floella: Skip Across the Ocean.
Nursery Rhymes from Around the World,
illustrated by Sheila Moxley
Frances Lincoln 1995 0711209669

BENNETT, Jill (editor): Tiny Tim, illustrated by
Helen Oxenbury
Mammoth 1993 0749709553

BENNETT, Jill (editor): People Poems,
illustrated by Nick Sharratt
Oxford University Press 1992 0192761102

BIRD, Michael (ed): The Grasshopper Laughs,
illustrated by Andrew Stooke
Faber 1995 0571175341/1996 0571179045

BLAKE, Quentin: All Join In
Cape 1990 0224027700/Red Fox 1992
0099964708/audio Tellastory 1992
1856562107

BLOOM, Valerie: Fruits, ilustrated by David
Axtell
Macmillan 1997 0333653114/0333653122

BRADMAN, Tony: Smile, Please! illustrated by
Jean Baylis
Puffin 1989 0140322868

CAUSLEY, Charles: "Quack!" said the Billy-
Goat, illustrated by Barbara Firth
Walker 1997 074455246X

COOK, Helen/Morag STYLES: Cambridge
Poetry Box 1
Class Library Pack A. Cambridge University
Press 1991 0521406552

ECCLESHARE, Julia (editor): First Poems,
illustrated by Selina Young
Orchard 1993/1996
1852134119/1852139560

EDWARDS, Richard: Moon Frog, illustrated
by Sarah Fox-Davies
Walker 1992/1996 0744521572/0744531616

FOREMAN, Michael: Mother Goose
Walker 1991 0744507758

FOSTER, John (editor): Dragon Poems,
illustrated by Korky Paul
Oxford University Press 1993 0192761080

HALLWORTH, Grace: Down by the River,
illustrated by Caroline Binch
Heinemann 1996 0434972312/Mammoth
1997 0749730250

JAMES, Frances (editor): The Cambridge Big
Book of Nursery Rhymes, illustrated by
Anthony Lewis (Cambridge Reading)
Cambridge University Press 1996
0521555574

KAUFMAN, William: Catch Me the Moon
Daddy
Kingscourt 1991 Available in big book format
plus pack of four small books plus audiotape

LEAR, Edward: The Jumblies, illustrated by
Emily Bolam
Orchard 1993 1852135131

LEAR, Edward: The Owl and the Pussycat,
illustrated by Louise Voce
Walker 1991/1993 0744512832/0744531217

MATTERSON, Elizabeth (editor): This Little
Puffin: Finger Plays and Nursery Games
Puffin 1991 0140340483

NETTELL, Stephanie (ed): Collins Treasury of
Poetry, illustrated by Penny Dann
HarperCollins 1995 0001939467

NICHOLLS, Sue: Bobby Shaftoe, Clap Your
Hands
A & C Black 1992 0713635568

NICHOLS, Grace: Asana and the Animals: A
Book of Pet Poems, illustrated by Sarah
Adams
Walker 1997 0744537401

OPIE, Iona: I Saw Esau, illustrated by Maurice
Sendak
Walker 1992 0744521513

OPIE, Iona: My Very First Mother Goose,
illustrated by Rosemary Wells
Walker 1996 0744544009

ORAM, Hiawyn (editor): Out of the Blue:
Stories and Poems about Colour, illustrated
by David McKee
Andersen Press 1992 0862643848 Picture
Lions 1994 0006643329

RICE, John: Bears Don't Eat Bananas,
illustrated by Charles Fuge
Macdonald Young Books 1991 0750004452

ROSEN, Michael (ed): Poems for the Very
Young, illustrated by Bob Graham

ROSEN, Michael (ed): A Spider Bought a
Bicycle, illustrated by Inga Moore
Kingfisher 1992 0862728746

ROSEN, Michael: We're Going on a Bear
Hunt, illustrated by Helen Oxenbury
Walker 1989/1993 0744511356/0744523230
Also in mini edition, big book & board book
formats

SANJEEVINI: Itchyka-dana. Asian Nursery
Rhymes
Mantra 1995 1852692340 Available on
cassette

STEVENSON, Robert Louis: A Child's Garden
of Verses
Gollancz 1996 057506286X (illustrated by
Michael Foreman)

Pavilion 1995 1857934830 (illustrated by
Joanna Isles)
Puffin 1995 014036692X

UMANSKY, Kaye: Three Singing Pigs: Making
Music with Traditional Stories
A & C Black 1994 0713642815

WALKER Book of First Rhymes
Walker 1996 0744544505

WRIGHT, Kit: Hot Dog
Puffin 1982 0140313362

KS2

AGARD, John (ed); Why is the Sky? illustrated by Andrzej Klimowski
Faber 1996 0571176860

AGARD, John/Grace NICHOLS (editors): A Caribbean Dozen, illustrated by Cathie Felstead
Walker 1994/1996 0744521726/074455201X

AHLBERG, Allan: Please Mrs Butler, illustrated by Fritz Wegner
Viking 1985 067080617X Puffin 1984 0140314946

ANGELOU, Maya: Life Doesn't Frighten Me at All, illustrated by Jean-Michel Basquiat
Stewart, Tabori & Chang 1993 1556702884

BERRY, James (ed): Classic Poems to Read Aloud
Kingfisher 1995/1997 1856972534/0753401207

BERRY, James: Playing a Dazzler
Hamish Hamilton 1996 0241135761/Puffin 1997 0140378316

BLAKE. Quentin (editor): Book of Nonsense Verse
Viking 1994 0670852287/Puffin 1996 0140366601

BLOOM, Valerie: Duppy Jamboree and other Jamaican Poems
Cambridge University Press 1992 0521380413/0521409092

BROWNING, Robert: The Pied Piper of Hamelin, illustrated by Andre Amstutz
Orchard 1994 1852136510

BURGHIE, Irving: Caribbean Carnival: Songs of the West Indies, illustrated by Frane Lessac
Macmillan 1993 0333605071

CAUSLEY, Charles: Going to the Fair, illustrated by Lianne Payne
Viking 1994 0670855650/Puffin 1996 0140369902

CHARLES, Faustin: Caribbean Counting Book, illustrated by Roberta Arenson
Barefoot 1996 1898000891

COOK, Helen/Morag STYLES: Cambridge Poetry Boxes 2 and 3
Class Library Pack B. Cambridge University Press 1991 0521406560

Class Library Pack C. Cambridge University Press 1991 0521406579

DAVIS, Carl/Hiawyn ORAM: A Creepy Crawly Songbook, illustrated by Satoshi Kitamura
Andersen Press 1993 0862643619

DOUTHWAITE, Gina: Picture a Poem
Hutchinson 1994 0091765404 Red Fox 1996 0099320711

GREENFIELD, Eloise/Jan Spivey GILCHRIST: Nathaniel Talking
Black Butterfly 1993 0863162002

GUNNING, Monica: Not a Copper Penny in Me House, illustrated by Frane Lessac
Macmillan 1995 0333618297

HARRISON, Michael/Christopher STUART-CLARK (eds): The Oxford Book of Story Poems
OUP 1995 019276103X

HARVEY, Anne (editor) : He Said, She Said, They Said: Poetry in Conversation
Puffin 1995 0140368124

HEANEY, Seamus/Ted HUGHES (editors): The School Bag
Faber 1997 0571177506/0571177514

HUGHES, Ted: Season Songs
Faber 1985 0571137032

HUTH, Angela (editor): Casting a Spell, illustrated by Jane Ray

Orchard 1996 1860390129

KAY, Jackie: Two's Company, illustrated by Shirley Tourret
Puffin 1992 014036952X

LONGFELLOW, Henry Wadsworth: Hiawatha's Childhood, illustrated by Errol Le Cain
Puffin 1986 140505628

McCLURE, Gillian (editor): I Can Move the Sea: 100 Poems by Children
Pont Books 1996 1859022790

McCLURE, Gillian (editor): Poems that Go Bump in the Night
Macdonald 1994 075001430X/0750014318

McGOUGH, Roger: Sky in the Pie, illustrated by Satoshi Kitamura
Puffin 1985 0140316124

McNAUGHTON, Colin: Have You Seen Who's Just Moved in Next Door to Us?
Walker 1991/1993 07445519497/0744530431

MITCHELL, Adrian (editor): The Orchard Book of Poems, illustrated by Chloe Cheese
Orchard 1996 1860392687

MITCHELL, Adrian (editor): Thirteen Secrets of Poetry
Macdonald 1993 0750013796/075001380X

MORGENSTERN, Christian: Lullabies, Lyrics and Gallows Songs, illustrated by Lisbeth Zwerger, translated from German by Anthea Bell
North-South Books 1995 1558583645

NICHOLLS, Judith (editor): Wordspells, illustrated by Alan Baker
Faber 1993 0571169090

NICHOLS, Grace: Give Yourself a Hug, illustrated by Kim Harley
A & C Black 1994 0713640545/Puffin 1996 0140372180

NICHOLS, Grace (editor): Can I Buy a Slice of Sky? Poems from Black, Asian and American Indian Cultures
Blackie 1991 0216930901

Hodder Knight 1993 0340588284

NOYES, Alfred: The Highwayman, illustrated by Charles Keeping
OUP 1981/1983 019272133X

PATTEN, Brian: Gargling with Jelly, illustrated by David Mostyn
Puffin 1986 0140319042

PRELUTSKY, Jack: The New Kid on the Block, illustrated by James Stevenson
Mammoth 1991 0749706023

PRELUTSKY, Jack (editor): The Walker Book of Poetry for Children, illustrated by Arnold Lobel
Walker 1983 0744502241

ROBERTS, Susan (editor): I'd Like to be a
Teabag
BBC 1991 0563362162

ROSEN, Michael: Don't Put Mustard in the
Custard, illustrated by Quentin Blake
Andre Deutsch 1996 0590542362

ROSEN, Michael (editor): The Kingfisher
Book of Children's Poetry
Kingfisher 1991 0862727847

ROSEN, Michael (ed): Walking the Bridge of
Your Nose: Wordplay, Poems and Rhymes,
illustrated by Chloe Cheese
Kingfisher 1997 0753401495

ROSEN, Michael: World of Poetry
Kingfisher 1995 1856974804/1994
1856972216

SHAKESPEARE, William: Something Rich and
Strange. A Treasury of Shakespeare's Verse,
selected by Gina Pollinger, illustrated by
Emma Chichester Clark
Kingfisher 1995 1856973875

STEWART, Pauline: Singing Down the
Breadfruit, illustrated by Duncan Smith
Bodley Head 1993 0370318242/Red Fox
1994 0099288214

STYLES, Morag/Susanna STEELE (editors):
Mother Gave a Shout, illustrated by Jane Ray
A & C Black 1990 0713632429

TENNYSON, Alfred, Lord: The Lady of
Shalott, illustrated by Charles Keeping
Oxford University Press 1989 0192722115

WEBB, Kaye (editor): I Like This Poem,
illustrated by Anthony Maitland
Puffin 1979 0140312951

ZEPHANIAH, Benjamin: Talking Turkeys
Viking 1994 0670847860 Puffin 0140363300

Acknowledgments

We thank all the contributors' schools
for permission to publish the
children's poems included in this
book.

We also thank the following schools
for permission to use photographs of
their classrooms:

Barlby Primary School

Rotherhithe Primary School

English Martyrs Primary School

Penwortham Primary School

Southfield Primary School

Longshaw Primary School

We thank Brenda Hockley and Iris
Scott (CLPE) for their work on the
manuscript and Ann Lazim (CLPE) for
her work on the bibliography.